PRAISE FOR *FAILURE IS NOT NOT AN OPTION*

"*Failure Is Not NOT an Option* is the real deal. One of life's great lessons is to never give up on yourself, and this book is that mantra personified. Patrick's honesty, huge heart, and humor shine through. It's a great read that will leave you uplifted and inspired."

—Bridget Everett, actress, comedian, singer, and star of HBO's *Somebody Somewhere*

"Patrick's story is just like the man himself: hilarious, loving, generous, exhausting, brilliant, endlessly entertaining, and ridiculously fun. He is living proof that every so-called failure is another chance to master something even more important: life."

—Martha Plimpton, Emmy Award–winning actress and activist

"After reading *Failure Is Not NOT an Option*, I have a new mantra: WWPD (What Would Patrick Do?). Not all of us are blessed with the relentless, indefatigable, never-give-up gene that propelled Patrick to approach and conquer a less-than-welcoming world with his wonderfully open and vulnerable heart. But we can all take inspiration from this Energizer Bunny, bear of a man. Knowing Patrick, it's no surprise that his memoir is funny, funny, funny. What I didn't expect was to find myself cheering lustily for him as I approached the final pages of his deliciously entertaining, deeply personal book, with tears running down my cheeks."

—Eric Marcus, founder and host of the award-winning *Making Gay History* podcast

"I cannot count the number of times I laughed out loud reading Patrick's hilarious, heartfelt memoir, and my amazement at learning we had so much in common. Early, doomed career delivering newspapers? Check. Twirling like Wonder Woman in times of stress? Check. Being an absolutely adorable, chubby dork with a crush on every boy within sight growing up? Check. Reading this book is like spending time with the sweetest, funniest friend you have and not wanting it to end. You'll find yourself rooting for Patrick through every failure, and falling in love with his big, gay heart."

—Rabia Chaudry, attorney and author of *Adnan's Story* and *Fatty Fatty Boom Boom*

FAILURE IS NOT NOT AN OPTION

How the Chubby Gay Son of a Jesus-Obsessed
Lesbian Found Love, Family, and Podcast
Success . . . and a Bunch of Other Stuff

PATRICK HINDS

with Doug Moe

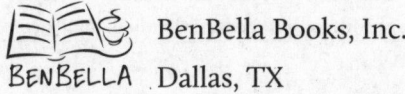

BenBella Books, Inc.
Dallas, TX

BENBELLA

BenBella Books, Inc.
10440 N. Central Expressway
Suite 800
Dallas, TX 75231
benbellabooks.com
Send feedback to feedback@benbellabooks.com

BenBella is a federally registered trademark.

Printed in the United States of America
10 9 8 7 6 5 4 3 2 1

Library of Congress Control Number: 2023004640
ISBN 9781637744253 (print)
ISBN 9781637744260 (ebook)

Editing by Alyn Wallace
Copyediting by Scott Calamar
Proofreading by Lisa Story and Madeline Grigg
Text design and composition by Aaron Edmiston
Cover design by Brigid Pearson
Cover image: Shutterstock / IS MODE (frame)
School photo on cover courtesy of the author
Printed by Lake Book Manufacturing

For Steve and Daisy, the loves of my life.

CONTENTS

OH, HEY!

Hi! I'm Patrick! Thanks for buying my book! I am for sure one of those psychos who punctuates just about every sentence with an exclamation point(!). If that's going to bother you, I hope it's not too late for you to return this! But if you *do* return this, I implore you to pick up a copy of *The Hours* by Michael Cunningham instead. It's great! And it's nothing like this book. *Very* few exclamation points!

Still here? YAY! Before we get much further, I should also warn you that I'm kind of a lot. But, like, in a fun way! According to my mother, I was Big Drama from the beginning. As she will lovingly tell anyone who will listen, I was born in the middle of a blizzard, in the middle of a rerun of Barbra Streisand's first TV special. She loves to frame this anecdote as if I picked that precise moment to extricate myself from her body in order to tell the world exactly what to expect from me. Forcing myself from her uterus in the middle of the worst weather event the country had seen in a generation meant that I'd be high maintenance. And the fact that I apparently popped myself out just in time for Babs's big finale, "Happy Days Are Here Again," most certainly meant that she'd also just delivered the world's newest homosexual—a fact that delighted her. In fact, so flaming gay was I right from the start that, according to the legend of my birth, I didn't make a single sound until Barbra hit the money note at the end of the song, at which point I burst into screams and tears.

"They were the shrieks of pure excitement and joy," my mother would say, really driving home the gay icon worship of it all.

"Are you sure it wasn't like the, you know, trauma of having just been born?" I would ask her. "Also, was there a TV in the delivery room? How were you *watching* that and giving birth to me at the same time?"

My mother never has good answers to these questions. She and I might share a slight penchant for hyperbole.

If you know anything about me at all, it might be that I co-host a pretty popular podcast called *True Crime Obsessed*. I'm one of the lucky few who has found a way to make a living making a podcast. I have a job I love and a family I love and so, in a lot of ways, I have, somehow, "made it." Which is weird because before that, I failed at many, many things. My life has been a series of fiascos, missteps, and just plain bad ideas. As an eternal optimist, I've always thrown myself into everything I've done, even when I probably shouldn't have. I devoted myself to becoming an actor even though I was terrible, I started a daycare even though I hated kids, and somehow I had a disastrous time with gay icon and former Golden Girl Bea Arthur, even though I couldn't be gayer.

But I guess by trying, and yes, failing at so many things, I finally found my way—to a great career, a great husband, and a great family.

Even to Broadway! I guess that's what this book is about: failure. But also succeeding by failing. Or failing while succeeding. Or maybe it's about finding myself? . . . Anyway, we'll see! And I promise there will be lots of exclamation points along the way. (!!!)

Chapter One

WORKING HARDER WHEN "SMARTER" ISN'T AN OPTION

In the spring of 1990, when I was twelve years old, I walked right past a dead body in the woods behind my house, but somehow completely missed it. I wish I could say that this was my true crime podcasting origin story, but no, it was just another sign that I'm not the world's most attentive person.

I must have passed the body a little after five in the morning, when I had just finished my paper route. At the time, we lived in a place called Swan Pond Village, a government-subsidized housing development—the poor section of our otherwise middle-class town on Cape Cod. And because most kids are assholes, those of us who grew up there got a lot of shit. My sister Becca, younger than me by just a year, got it especially bad. One of the most memorable, and, with the benefit of hindsight, straight-up hilarious pieces of bullying my sister endured came at the hands of her classmate Dave O'Riley. Dave was a ratty little skater punk—totally my type—and an extremely talented artist. You'd think this hot little artsy freak would have been our people! But nope, the kid was a dick. Anyway, each little neighborhood in our housing project had a community dumpster. On the front of each dumpster was a sticker with the letters BFI—the initials of the sanitation company that owned it. So one day, hot brilliant artist Dave whipped up and widely circulated (!) an original piece: a drawing of one of these dumpsters with my entire family's faces peeking out from the inside. And filling in the letters of the BFI sticker on the front of the dumpster, he wrote:

BECCA'S

FAMILY

INSIDE.

If you are doubled over in laughter or just did a spit take of some kind, I want you to know that you should not feel bad. Even though almost every time I've told this story, it's been with a chuckle, I've been admonished that it's actually cruel and not funny . . . but Becca and I both still find it hilarious, which is why I keep telling it. Also, through a recent Google search, I learned that Dave O'Riley is dead, so really my family had the last laugh. Just kidding. Dave is fine. But he *is* way less hot now, so still a win for us.

Anyway, I didn't hear about the body in the woods until after school a day after breezing past it. The friendly neighborhood police officer—a hot twentysomething we called Officer Nick, who is definitely responsible for a minor men-in-uniform fetish that lives rent-free in my brain—was talking with our neighbor Jennifer.

"What was all the commotion down by the pond this morning?" Jennifer asked. Incidentally, Jennifer's live-in boyfriend, Matthew, was a construction worker who would sometimes unzip his full-body jumpsuit and just let the top part dangle, leaving him naked from the waist up. A practice which . . . did not bother me at all. Looking back now, I realize two things: One, I was a very horny twelve-year-old. And two, with Officer Nick and construction worker Matthew, my neighborhood crushes were just a biker, a cowboy, and an Indian shy of being the Village People. Which totally tracks.

"We pulled a dead body down from a tree," said Officer Nick.

"Oh my God," Jennifer said. "Where?"

"Right at the top of the walking trail. The poor bastard was dangling *over* the trail. From the looks of it, he'd been there all night."

This stopped me cold. "He was there all night?" I asked.

"At least," Officer Nick said.

This was . . . concerning. The entirety of Swan Pond Village is about three-quarters of a mile long, and behind the line of houses is a thick forest, with the titular Swan Pond in its middle. The way my paper route was . . . routed . . . I would start at one end of the neighborhood and finish at the other. And the fastest way to get home once I'd delivered all the papers—usually at around 5 AM—was to walk down to the pond and then up through the woods on the trail to my back door.

Being a parent myself now, I have to question my mother's wisdom in allowing me to do this at that age. Like, I get it: twelve-year-olds have paper routes, it's a rite of passage or whatever, but the walk home, *through the pitch-black forest (!?!)*, all by myself at five in the morning . . . sounds like something a parent should have advised against? Then again, maybe she was *hoping* I'd get kidnapped or murdered?

At twelve, I was a very big eater and my family was living on a fixed income, so this is all starting to make sense.

But if what Officer Nick was saying was true—and the very newspaper I delivered the next day would confirm that it *was*—and this dead body had been hanging above the entrance to the trail since sometime last night, then, I, on my way home, would have Walked. Directly. Under. The. Body.

This, it turns out, was my "indoor kid" origin story.

. . . .

This story has so many of the elements that would feature prominently later in my life: true crime, a general obliviousness to the world around me, money problems, and musical theater. Oh yes, musical theater. Because you see, I wasn't working as a paperboy just to earn a little walking-around money, like most paperboys. And it wasn't, strictly speaking, because we were poor, though that was part of it. No, I was risking life and limb in the woods at 5 AM because I was determined to become a Newsie.

Earlier that year I had seen the Disney movie musical *Newsies* about the 1901 newspaper boy strike, and like any twelve-year-old, musical-theater-addicted, horny-homosexual-preteen, I was completely obsessed. The singing! The dancing! The boys running around their "orphans' home" in just their underpants! Sure, twelve-year-old me liked looking at them, but mostly I wanted to *be* them. I begged my mother for dance classes, voice classes, a n y t h i n g classes that would help release my Inner Newsie. But being as poor as we were, there was absolutely no way. Unless I got some kind of job. So when my neighbor Luke gave up his paper route, I jumped at the opportunity. I was killing two birds with one stone. I thought I could earn who could blame him? But when he was finished with the quart, he would just toss the empty container into any vacant corner of the car where it would rest forever among the pile of previously discarded candy bar wrappers and pretzel bags. Is this description of my dad's filthy car relevant to the story? Not really. I'm mostly just writing this for my husband, Steve, to explain that slovenliness is in my DNA, so maybe he should go a little bit easier on me.

We were about twenty minutes into the ride to my father's house when he announced that we'd need to stop at a Goodwill someplace to get us some clothes.

"Why?" my sister Sarah asked. As the oldest, she was naturally sitting in the front seat.

My father hesitated, which is what caught my attention and made me start actually listening.

"Because you're going to live with me now," he said, with not a lot of confidence.

"Pfffft, no we're not," Sarah blurted out, instantly—and hilariously—emasculating our father with a snort and three one-syllable words. She was fourteen.

My dad paused again. He did not have a plan for this. How to counter the scathing skepticism that tween girls wield so effectively? She had barely looked up from the magazine she was leafing through.

"Yes . . . you are?" he said, sort of as a question. "If that woman thinks she's getting a dime out of me, she has another think coming. You're going to live with ME and she can pay ME child support."

Sarah thought for a second, and then said, "Wait, are you seriously kidnapping us right now?" She was not afraid. She said this with a genuine mixture of curiosity and amusement. This had finally gotten more interesting than her magazine.

"Uhhhhh," my father stammered.

She waited to see if he had anything else to say and then said, "Okay, so you can bring us back now, or I can jump out of this car right here in the middle of the highway."

"Sarah don't be ridic—WAIT, WHAT ARE YOU DOING?" he yelled, as Sarah rolled down her window, blasting us all with cold New England air. We were going about sixty miles per hour. She stuck her arms out the window and started waving them at the car in the lane next to ours.

"SARAH, STOP IT RIGHT NOW!" my father shouted. The poor bastard was panicking.

The woman in the car next to us did a double take and then rolled down her own window, mouthing the words "Are you okay?"

And then Sarah, her voice dripping with boredom, and punctuated with what I can only imagine was an epic eye roll, started yelling, "THIS MAN IS KIDNAPPING USSSSSS!"

"OH FOR CHRIST'S SAKE," my father screamed. "ROLL THE WINDOW UP AND I'LL TAKE YOU HOME."

Next-lane-over lady, having not heard my sister because we were all going *sixty miles per hour*, shook her head, mouthing, "What? WHAAAAA?"

Sarah just waved, gave her a thumbs-up, and went back to her magazine. My dad got off at the next exit and we were home less than an hour after he picked us up. It might have been the world's shortest, and laziest, kidnapping attempt.

. . . .

We didn't see a whole lot of my dad after this, and we certainly didn't see any of that child-support money. So into the workforce we went.

Sarah was fourteen, so she could work, like, legally. And this was Cape Cod, so there was no end of shitty T-shirt stands and frozen yogurt carts that were happy to throw her five dollars an hour. But I was still underage for most real jobs, and one near miss with a human corpse was enough to put an end to my newspaper-delivery career.

I'd heard through friends at school that a local tourist attraction called the Family Farm would hire underage kids for the summer and pay them cash under the table. Even better, the place was within bike-riding distance from my house. "The Family Farm" sounds wholesome, but it was the kind of place that no local ever went to. The entrance was set back several hundred feet from the main road and, from the outside, the whole place looked dark and sort of scary. (Also, didn't Charles Manson call his ranch the "Family Farm"?) Arguably, this place had a much more murder-y vibe than the Swan Pond Village walking path, but I didn't care. I had tap classes to pay for. I would have helped the owners perform ritual human sacrifices if it meant having the money to learn to time step.

After a brief interview, I was hired on the spot. I was told to arrive for my first day of work at seven in the morning. Early, yes, but compared to my newspaper job's 4 AM wake-up time, a luxuriously late start.

Upon my arrival, Danny, one of the owners, walked me down to the petting zoo, a main attraction at the farm. This petting zoo was huge, maybe a third of a football field, and was home to all kinds of barnyard animals—goats, sheep, chicken, pigs—who just roamed freely within the confines, rolling around in the mud and eating their own shit. As we approached, the smell hit me. *Oh my GOD*, I thought, *had one of them died?* Having narrowly avoided a *human* body on my paper route, was I now about to have to deal with a rotting fucking pig corpse? I wasn't ready for this. I just needed to earn money for my poor family, and for dancing and singing lessons. My stomach started to turn. *Jesus, how long has that thing been dead*, I wondered as I instinctively covered my nose and mouth. I looked up at Danny, fully expecting him to break into a sprint, kick the gate open, and find that poor dead son of a bitch. Instead, he just stared back at me blankly. Then he got annoyed. "Haven't you ever smelled a FARM before?" he sneered.

It took me a second to process that there was no rotting carcass. This was just what this place smelled like. All the time.

Danny shoved a large yard rake into my hand and said, "I need you to rake all the animal shit into one corner and then shovel it into a barrel. We open in an hour, so chop-chop." And with that, he turned and walked away. This seemed like an impossible, not to mention fucking disgusting, task. Also, if I cleaned up all the shit, what would the animals eat all day?

I should have just left right then; I mean, we all see where this is going, right? But you have to understand: I had visions of dance shoes in my head. So I grabbed the rake and walked into the pen. Instantly, I was assaulted—yes, I said *assaulted*—by a stampede of starving, sticky, grunting, mouth-breathing creatures. Before we go any further, I want to be clear that I do not blame these animals for being disgusting, for stinking, for living just to smell each other's butts or eat their own shit. Animals gonna animal. These filthy animals were living their best goddamn lives. I just wanted them off of me. So I did the only thing I could think of: I screamed in as high a pitch as I could muster and spun around clumsily like Wonder Woman. The animals backed off immediately, and I swear I could see pity in their fuzzy faces.

Things did not improve when I started raking. Probably assuming I was there to feed them, the animals followed me wherever I went. How many times could I whirl like Lynda Carter? I just had to rake and hope that they'd grow bored of me. But they grew more aggressive. When I didn't present them with food, the goats started chewing on my shoelaces and the bottom of my T-shirt. I'd shoo them away just as a larger lamb or another fucking goat—WHAT ON EARTH IS THE DIFFERENCE??—would jump up on me, putting two legs on my shoulders and its wet, slimy snout in my face. The slow-moving, relentless push of these animals felt like a goddamn zombie apocalypse, and I fully expected that once they were done with my shoes and shirt, I'd be eaten alive.

It was when I heard myself making terrified gay grunts—it's the combination of breathiness and high pitch that makes these grunts singularly homosexual, in case you were wondering—that I knew I wasn't going to last. And I want to be clear: I'm not afraid of hard work. In fact, I've always prided myself on my work ethic, and I push myself to the limits of my abilities; it's just that sometimes . . . I don't have much ability. And I'm not necessarily prissy, either; I have no problem getting my hands dirty. But there was something about this combination of filthy animals, poop, the stench of, like, the *outside*, and the heat that was just too unbearable. Even for this little queen who thought he would have done anything to learn to dance like a Newsie.

Somehow, someway, I made it to the end of that day. After hauling goat feed, cleaning rabbit cages, and then going back to raking animal shit until I could barely stand, I finished the day by leading pony rides on a grumpy old horse named Cinnamon. Cinnamon, incidentally, gave off very strong lesbian energy, so you'd think we'd have gotten along. But nope, she bit me twice and then kicked a pig in front of a group of waiting children, I swear to God, just to make them cry.

At the end of the day, the owner handed me a twenty-dollar bill. A. TWENTY. DOLLAR. BILL. For eleven hours of work. I folded the money and put it in my pocket knowing I would not be coming back. To nobody's surprise, farm life was not for me.

· ·

By the summer between eighth and ninth grade, I was finally old enough to get a real job. My sister Sarah's boyfriend, Joey, was a line cook at a restaurant in a beachfront hotel called the Red Jacket Inn in the fancy part of town. Everyone in my family was obsessed with Joey, even my mother. We all still talk about him to this day. At seventeen years old, he was tough, a little mean, and very, very cool. So when he asked me if I wanted to work as a dishwasher at the restaurant, I jumped at the chance. ANYTHING that would make him like me better.

Restaurant kitchens have a reputation for being intimidating places to work. They're hot, cramped, full of machines that burn or cut you, and are almost always staffed by arrogant, macho, straight men. The kitchen at Red Jacket was no exception. The assortment of characters who worked there, at least in their own minds, were all tough, "manly" men. And this is where I feel the need to address one strange and fascinating thing that I'd come to learn was a cornerstone of restaurant kitchen culture: These guys can't keep their hands off each other. Like, sexually. I mean, I guess I don't doubt that all of these men are heterosexual if they say they are, but the sheer amount of ass grabbing, crotch groping, pretend humping, and just plain over-the-clothes handsiness I saw in that and *every kitchen I've ever worked in* is astounding.

But like I said, this was a "man's world," and it was not a given that I'd be accepted. Joey's stamp of approval was great, but he'd be cooking dinners and I was the morning guy, so he wouldn't be around to defend me. I was grateful then that on the first morning of work, the head chef, Bob Smith, met me with a warm and jolly welcome, "Hey, heyyyy! You must be Joey's guy." Bob, who had to be pushing sixty-five, stood no taller than five feet and was always dressed head to toe in uniform kitchen whites, including a Pillsbury Doughboy–style chef's hat and a white kerchief around his neck. He was an avid smoker and had a mouth full of yellowing teeth to show for it.

"Yes, I am!" I said, excited to get going. The place smelled like a combination of corned beef hash, pancakes, and coffee. Ahhh, the smells of the inside. I was already feeling at home.

Bob walked me into the kitchen to meet Travis Johnson, the head dishwasher. Travis, of course, needed no introduction. He was a junior at my high school and a star athlete. He was popular and gorgeous—six feet tall, blond, slender, muscular. Standing in his presence, in the cramped kitchen of the Red Jacket Inn, I was starstruck and a little bit speechless.

"Travis, this is Patrick," Bob said.

Travis didn't say anything. He seemed unimpressed.

"He's Joey's kid. Be nice to him," Bob said, before turning and walking away.

Travis thought for a second. Then he asked, "You like getting dirty, Billy?"

"Oh, um, it's Patrick," I said, shyly.

"I'm gonna call you Billy," he said.

"Oh, okay," I said. *WAS HE FLIRTING?*

"There's this cartoon I like," he explained. "It's about a little donkey named Billy who eats everything around him. Not just food, but like, tables, trees, cars. Everything."

"Uh-huh," I said, lost in his big, beautiful eyes.

"You look like you like to eat too. So I'm gonna call you Billy."

Reader, I swear to God, he wasn't being mean. He was being hot and tall and dumb and using word association to remember what to call me. Call me Patrick, call me Billy, just call me!

"Do you like getting dirty, Billy?" he repeated, as he walked me over to one of the sinks.

"I don't mind getting dirty," I said. And it was true! I lived my life in stained clothes. Slovenliness! It's in my DNA, *Steve*.

"Good," Travis said. "If you don't mind getting dirty, you're gonna be great at this job. Your first task is the poaching pan." He then handed me a contraption that was a cross between a skillet and a pot. I'd come to learn that the cooks filled this thing with water and kept it at a low boil throughout breakfast service to poach eggs in. By that point, the inside bottom of this thing was a stark black color. Travis turned on the water, handed me a scrub brush and walked away.

This was a test, and I was determined to pass it. I made the water as hot as I could take and started to scrub at the black residue. Nothing. I added dish soap and scrubbed again. Nothing—the bottom was still jet-black. Dishes started to pile up in the sink as the cooks unloaded their breakfast cookware. I was getting nervous; this was taking too long.

Maybe I'd misunderstood? No amount of scrubbing seemed to make a difference. It seemed like the bottom of the poaching pan was just . . . black? I walked over to Travis, trying to be casual.

"How's it going, Billy?" he asked.

"Well, I've been scrubbing and scrubbing, but it doesn't seem like I can get anything off."

"Oh sure you can, Billy," he said. "You just gotta use some elbow grease."

"OH!" I said, genuinely grateful. I *knew* there had to be a reasonable explanation. "Okay, well, where do we keep it?" I asked.

Travis looked confused, which in turn confused me. Shit! Had he shown me and I'd forgotten?

"You want to know where we keep the . . . elbow grease?" he asked.

"Yeah!" I said. "I knew I was missing something."

"Um, you know, I'm not sure where we keep it now," he said with a sly smile. "Ask Bob, he'll know."

"Great!" I said, as I trotted off to find the boss.

Look, I know most of you have heard of "elbow grease." And I can't really explain why I'd never heard the term before. It's one of those weird holes in my knowledge at the time that is too specific to be a lie. It's like how you mishear a lyric to a song and only find out that Fiona Apple is in fact *not* wailing "BASTARD, YOU ARE A BASTARD" in "Fast as You Can" when your best friend Mike overhears you singing it and then laughs and points at you in a room full of your mutual friends. Also, how has no one invented and bottled a high-powered cleaning agent and called it Elbow Grease? Seems like a missed opportunity to me.

Anyway, I found Bob in his office.

"Joey's kid! How's it going?" he asked, a cigarette dangling from his mouth.

"Good!" I said. And now was my chance to show him that I was taking initiative. "Actually, I'm working on the poaching pan and

Travis said I needed to use some elbow grease, so I'm just trying to figure out where we keep it."

Bob just stared at me. And then he cracked a yellow-toothed smile. "Hey Johno," he shouted across the kitchen, "Joey's kid is working on the poaching pan and he's looking for the"—he stifled a laugh—"*elbow grease*. Where are we keeping that these days?"

Johno was Bob's number two in the kitchen. He was one of those hot-adjacent, twentysomething beach-town guys who peaked in high school and then sort of resigned themselves to not accomplishing much after that. But he seemed happy and took off his shirt a lot, so who was I to judge? Travis had already gotten to him, and they were both doubled over.

"You know, I'm not sure, Bob," Johno shouted back.

"You're just gonna have to look around for it, Billy!" Travis chimed in.

And so I did. For the next thirty minutes, I searched every shelf, closet, and cabinet in that kitchen. I was going to find the goddamned elbow grease if it killed me. Then I'd be able to clean the pan *and* let the rest of the team know what had become of this very valuable cleaning solution. I was going to prove myself to be indispensable.

Eventually, one of the waitresses took pity on me. "They're messing with you," she whispered, as she walked past me. I was shoulder deep in the baking cabinet. "It's an *expression*. It means 'put some muscle into it.'"

I froze. I could feel Travis's, Johno's, and Bob's eyes on me. And this is where something truly unexpected happened: I laughed. I knew I was supposed to feel humiliated . . . but I didn't. And that surprised even me. Maybe I'm romanticizing things, but I remember this as a big moment of realization for me. A lot of thoughts bombarded me all at once: First of all, the prank was hilarious—and harmless—so why *not* laugh? Also, I really *wanted* this job, so what good would it do for me to get offended and, what—like cry or yell or something? And wait! Oh my Goddess, WHY NOT APPLY THIS TO LIFE? *Just take shit less seriously to get the things you want!* Okay, fine; that last one took much longer to internalize. But truly, learning that being "in on the joke" was one way to survive in the world was a true revelation for me. And it definitely felt like the right thing for the moment.

Stifling my laugh, I turned around and did a walk of shame back to the sink. I tried to act sad and confused and embarrassed—I wanted to give the guys that. They'd earned it. Later they'd tell me that they half expected me to burst into tears and run out the back door. Instead, I proved that there was a place in this macho kitchen for a lovable, effeminate doof.

I turned the water on as hot as I could make it, picked up the scrub brush, leaned all my body weight into it, and scrubbed like my life depended on it. When the caked-on black grit on the bottom of the pan started to give way, I pushed even harder. It took me fifteen minutes to get the thing clean, but when I was finished, to quote the musical *Annie*, because I. Am. That. Gay: the thing "shined like the top of the Chrysler Building."

Bob walked over as I was hanging the thing up to dry. "Well shit," he said. "Look who found the elbow grease."

. . . .

I worked in the kitchen at the Red Jacket Inn for seven (very gay) straight summers, which is the longest I've ever had any job. In my time there, I was everything from a dishwasher to a prep cook to the *head breakfast chef*, which honestly just means that you're the one who gets yelled at if the pancakes get served cold. I loved it there for so many reasons, but mostly because I was constantly surprising myself. I found that I could be tough—not in a stupid, macho, strongman kind of way—but in my work ethic and stamina. No, I wouldn't have survived seven summers of stinking, rotting animals at the Family Farm, but somehow making five hundred breakfasts and lunches in a 110-degree kitchen on my feet in front of a blazing oven for eight straight hours suited me just fine. I worked for years alongside guys I came to love who I never would have talked to—and who never would have talked to me—in real life.

My last day at the Red Jacket Inn was at the end of the summer between my freshman and sophomore years of college. When my shift was over, Bob told me he wanted to talk to me. He pulled me into the back hallway by the punch clock where he took people when they needed a serious talking-to.

"Billy," he said (yeah, that nickname never went away), "you know I love you very much." *Oh my God,* I thought, *this old fucker is about to cry.*

"I love you too, Bob, you old, crying queer," I said. Bob wiped his eyes and then shrieked with laughter. Bob loooooooooved a gay joke.

"Seriously, though, Billy," he continued. "I just wanted to say, we have been very accepting of your lifestyle. And I wanted to warn you that . . . um . . . other people may not be so accepting. So, be safe, and be careful out there."

The little old man with the yellow teeth and kerchief around his neck and the silly little Pillsbury Doughboy hat, who probably had had deep reservations about hiring me all those years ago, smiled up at me. He was quite proud of himself for being so progressive. I was proud of him too.

"Thank you, Bob," I said. I leaned in and gave him a hug. And then I whispered in his ear, "Now I'm gonna go tell everyone you brought me back here and asked for a blow job."

"HAHAHAHAHAHAHAHAH," Bob wheeze-laughed as he hugged me back.

Chapter Two

SMALL PART. BIG ACTOR.

icture it: the Dennis-Yarmouth Regional High School chorus room. Spring 1996. Among the music stands, instruments, and props, a group of young thespians stretch and shake out their hands. They roll their shoulders and vocalize in preparation. Today is the day. The most important day of my senior year, maybe the most important day of my entire life: audition day for the spring musical, *Bye Bye Birdie*.

Everyone who was anyone in my high school's drama club was there:

Trilling softly in the corner was Scene-Stealing Legend, Kate. In the previous year's production of *Oklahoma!*, she had been cast in a nonspeaking ensemble role, but over the course of the six-month rehearsal process, she had managed to give her character a name—"Donna"—*and* several unwritten, scene-stealing lines. These included, but were not limited to, a center-stage moment during a fight between the characters Ado Annie and Gertie in which she pulled focus by shouting, "YOU GET THAT HUSSIE, ADO ANNIE!" *and then fainted*. Kate was a force. Some people said that Donna was their favorite character, even though she didn't even have her own credit in the program.

My acting arch-nemesis, Christian, was there too, casually doodling in a notebook. He had all the unearned confidence and swagger of a good-looking, straight, upper-middle-class white kid, and I resented the hell out of him. Didn't he understand that theater was for the *freaks?* If any old handsome, confident preppie could sing and dance, what the hell were *we* supposed to do? Play lacrosse? In fairness to Christian, he and I would go on to become very, very good friends once I realized that most of my resentment came from my wanting to bone him. But I digress; in that audition room, he was to be feared and hated.

Becca Hinds was there too—my devious, not-to-be-trusted sister. Yes, Becca was absolutely my best friend in the entire world, but that just made her betrayal of the previous year all the more hurtful. In that production of *Oklahoma!*, I'd been *this* close to nabbing the leading role of Will Parker, and everything was going smoothly until the girl they wanted to play my love interest quit the show. According to the director, Becca was the only girl left in the drama club—nay, the *entire school*—who could sing the role, and so he cast her as the replacement. And, *incredibly*, she actually took the part. Out of desperation, I pleaded with the director in front of the entire cast that the kissing scene wasn't necessarily a deal breaker for me—WE COULD MAKE IT WORK! But still, I was punted to the chorus. And guess who took over the role? Super-hot arch-nemesis Christian.

Quietly lurking in the corner, easily missed, was Jean-Luc. Very concerning. Jean-Luc was one of those kids who just kind of appeared in eighth grade. Every school has one of those kids. They just sort of *poof* in and you're like, *Huh? Was he always here? Is he new?* Nobody seemed to know. He was a quiet kid who floated through high school, not really making friends or causing any trouble, just being vaguely hot, vaguely French, but otherwise unmemorable. But it was this vagueness, this lack of definition that made him all the more dangerous, as we had found out the previous year at the Spring Talent Show.

This talent show was always a forgettable mess since I was the only person in my town with any *real* talent, and I would *never* deign to participate. Yes, I might have been an unbearable, insecure nightmare in high school. Anyway, that spring, my friends and I suffered through this cavalcade of non-stars until they made a surprising announcement: The final act of the Spring Talent Show would be . . . Jean-Luc. *Jean-Luc? The quiet kid with the ponytail that oddly works for him even though it definitely shouldn't?* And when we were told that he'd be singing Elvis Presley's "Hound Dog," I let out an audible "Oh no."

This was sure to be a debacle. I myself had lived through a humiliation like this once. In the Fifth Grade Talent Show, I sang the classic rock song "Jessie's Girl" by Rick Springfield. To add some flare, I did a side-to-side toe touch as I sang and built in some choreography to match the words. I'd practiced and practiced, and though I didn't really understand the lyrics about "feeling dirty," it seemed like an important part that I really needed to sell, so I belted them with exuberant prepubescent aplomb. I closed my eyes for dramatic effect and really tried to convey some emotion when I hit the pre-chorus: She watches him and then does . . . something . . . sexual (?) with her super-hot bod? So I gyrated my hips. And then, as the song goes, the two characters sort of smash their bodies together, so I mimed pulling a body into mine as I gyrated harder. I was practically grunting now. IT WAS ALL GOING SO WELL! When I opened my eyes to finish out the verse and take in the rapturous applause I had surely earned, I was shocked to find a stunned, utterly inert audience full of very confused elementary school children and—we'll use the word "concerned"—adult teachers.

Look: I like to take big swings. At home, in front of the mirror, I'd *become* Rick Springfield, pining for Jessie's girl; in front of the assembled fifth-grade students and teachers, that inner vision had somehow failed to translate. Instead of Rick Springfield's smoldering confidence and emotional vulnerability, the audience had seen the unfortunate reality. Do you remember that supercute little kid from *Jerry Maguire*? The one with the glasses and cute lisp who says, "Jerry, did you know the human head weighs eight pounds?" I kinda looked like that kid, but add forty pounds, swap out the adorable round glasses for Coke-bottle-thick D. B. Cooper glasses, and change the blond buzz cut to a brown-hair sprayed-on-top and blown-out-in-the-back mullet, fashioned after the one sported by my own middle-aged lesbian mother. Add a dash of Richard Simmons's flamboyant *Sweatin' to the Oldies* choreography, and there you had: Me! Let's just say that the audience's confusion—and *total* lack of applause—makes more sense to me now than it did then.

Back at the Spring Talent Show, I was sure that this same fate now awaited Jean-Luc. *Why would he do this to himself?* He was a year away from being completely forgotten by everyone who ever knew him in high school! And isn't that the best-case scenario for most of us? Sure, he hadn't made a splash, but he also hadn't had to live down any particular humiliations. He—an invisible French guy named Jean-Luc, with a goddamned ponytail—had miraculously gotten through the worst time in most peoples' lives without a debilitating trauma to work through in a lifetime of therapy. And now he was going to close out the junior year talent show by singing Elvis Fucking Presley?!? The poor guy. Also . . . this was gonna be hilarious.

Jean-Luc walked out onto the stage. IN. A. *SUIT*. *Oh my God*, I thought. *Here we go*. And then he started.

The bitchy gay bark-laugh caught in my throat. *W.A.I.T.*, I thought, as I grabbed my friend Alison's hand. *This can't be. This . . . is impossible. JEAN-LUC IS FUCKING FANTASTIC.*

Jean-Luc swiveled his hips and tossed the mic stand around, channeling the King of Rock and Roll himself. And like the King, he was sexy as *hell*. Wow. Everyone around us leapt to their feet. Boys who I'd personally witnessed shoving Jean-Luc into open classroom doors during passing periods were doing Arsenio Hall fist bumps in the air. Girls were literally fanning themselves. Jean-Luc had transformed the half-awake students of the Dennis-Yarmouth Regional High School auditorium into the manic teenage throngs of a 1950s *Ed Sullivan Show* audience. He brought the house down with such a frenzy that people were actually mad that he didn't have an encore. And Jean-Luc, wherever you are today, I hope that memory is your last thought every night before you go to bed. Because I'll tell you, I've never forgotten it. As someone who sought the same glory with Rick Springfield but came up short, I tip my hat to you, sir.

But *anyway*. In that audition room, Jean-Luc was the enemy. The thing was, there was a role in *Bye Bye Birdie* that was absolutely perfect for him, and it was the title character! The character Conrad Birdie was a young pop star based on ELVIS PRESLEY. It should have been a no-brainer to cast Dennis-Yarmouth Regional High School's own Elvis as Conrad. But in an act of true high school drama club some money for classes, but also hone my craft every morning by *becoming* a real-life Newsie. (It's called method acting, people.)

From as far back in my childhood as I can remember, anything I wanted, outside of the extreme basics, I needed to pay for myself. It's not that my mother didn't want to get us things; it's just that, after she left my father, extras were no longer an option.

My parents' divorce was finalized just before I turned eight. From then on, money was always a concern in my mom's house. Of course, my father could have made things easier for us by paying the court-ordered child support. But after losing his half-hearted custody battle, his bruised ego wouldn't allow it. And I have to say: in a way, it's still sort of remarkable that my mother got custody. Don't get me wrong; she was absolutely the right parent for us to be living with, but this was the late '80s—not exactly the most progressive of times. And my mom was now a poor, single, newly out-of-the-closet lesbian, who had just started Alcoholics Anonymous. So how unimpressive must my dad have been for the judge to look at him and think to himself, *Yeah, no, the kids are going with the boozy carpet muncher whose car has just been repossessed.*

Anyway, with the court breathing down my father's neck over his reluctance to make his support payments, on one of our weekend visits with him, things took a turn for the kidnappy. Yup, I was once kidnapped by my father. Ish.

Again, I was *this* close to a true crime origin story. But whereas I almost never give up when I should, my father has always been a quitter (except when it came to his carton-a-day smoking habit). On the Friday of my near kidnapping, he picked me and my three siblings up in his dirty Ford Escort. Just a quick aside about my father and his car: The man loved to drink chocolate milk by the quart, which, I mean, diva-dom so bold that you had to respect it, Jean-Luc _only agreed to audition if the role of Conrad Birdie was_ off _the table_. He was a serious actor, he'd told the director, and didn't want to be typecast.

Very noble. But I knew the real reason Jean-Luc didn't want to be cast as Conrad Birdie, and it had nothing to do with being an "artiste." The real reason was that _Bye Bye Birdie_ is one of the few shows where the title character, though definitely the most interesting, wasn't actually the _lead_ character. And as any drama club alum will tell you, high school acting is not about playing nuanced, layered roles; it's about having _the most lines_. If your highlighter isn't completely dry from marking up your script by the end of the first read-through, you have failed. Christian, Jean-Luc, and I were all there for one reason: to be cast as Albert, Conrad Birdie's completely bland and uninteresting talent agent who, somehow, gets all the songs and basically never leaves the stage. In other words: the Lead Character.

I knew all the tricks of this rogue's gallery. We were competitors, yes, but also recent collaborators. Christian, Jean-Luc, my traitorous sister Becca, scene-stealing Kate, and I had all done a play together earlier in the year. _The Way We Live Now_ by Susan Sontag was about a group of friends in 1980s New York City struggling to come to terms with the AIDS crisis as their friends all died around them. Think _Friends_, but without any of the comedy. As the gay kid of a lesbian mother who'd had friends literally die of the disease in her arms—and it being barely ten years after the events in the plot took place—I knew it was an important story. And I knew that Sontag was a "genius" and a "celebrated writer" and blah-blah-blah. But come on: as we traveled and competed with this important show (traveling competitive drama club—does it get any gayer?), all that we sixteen-year-olds _really_ cared about were all the dramatic tragedy-filled line readings we could wring out of the piece. And, boy, oh boy, was this play built to deliver!

First of all, the characters didn't have names; we were just "Voices 1–5." How perfectly over-the-top is that? Second, the dialogue wasn't linear. The whole play was just fragments of conversation, all of them delivered in the third person. For example:

> VOICE 1: *I was thinking, Ursula said to Quentin, that the difference between a story and a painting or a photograph is that in a story, you can write "he's still alive," but in a painting or a photograph you can't show "still." You can just show him being alive.*
> VOICE 2: *He's still alive, Steven said.*

Please, imagine this material in the hands of angsty, hormonal, attention-starved teenagers. Hell yes, we emoted. And we took this play all the way to the state finals, by the way. Because of course we did. I mean, what adult judge was going to vote against the woke AIDS play in 1996? On that trip to the state finals, Jean-Luc, Christian, and I had to share a hotel room with two double beds, which meant that two of us would have to double up. On the drive there, Christian asked me—in front of everyone—if I wanted to share a bed. He was 100 percent just being nice because he's an awesome guy—he'd thought ahead and was kindly allowing me to avoid the awkward "Who's gonna sleep in the same bed as the gay guy" moment. But it was all I could think about for the rest of the day. *Would we spoon? Would we get a little handsy after Jean-Luc fell asleep?* No, it turned out, we would not. But that wouldn't stop me from staying awake all night hoping for it!

I tell you all this because the experience of *The Way We Live Now* had forged a bond between us all and had solidified us into a true troupe of AC-TORS. And it showed me what I was up against with Christian and Jean-Luc in an audition situation. It's not that they were, like, great actors or anything, but our recent drama club victories had reinforced their natural-born heterosexual high school boy confidence. And they had proven that they met the criteria to carry on the age-old tradition of heterosexual high school boys stealing leading roles from flamboyant gay teens WHO WANTED IT MORE THAN THEY DID. Namely, they were alive, they could memorize most of their lines, and they could deliver those lines with an acceptable amount of projection. That was enough to crush any young queen's acting dreams.

We were thirty minutes into the audition, and both Christian and Jean-Luc had been called up to read for Albert. Whatever, they were fine. When the director called my name, I was ready. I'd rigorously prepared by watching the Dick Van Dyke movie version no fewer than ten times. I'd memorized the Albert audition scene *like a goddamn professional*. I was hydrated. I was about to *burn that place down* (with my charm).

As I stepped up to start the scene, Mr. Sadowski, our director, stopped me. "Patrick," he said, "you'll be reading for the role of Mr. MacAfee."

Mr. MacAfee. Mr. MacAfee? *Mr. MacAfee* was . . . not the lead.

An audible murmur arose among the other auditioners. All eyes were on me. Breaths were bated. Nobody knew how I might react. But I understood that I had to play it cool and appear unsurprised, like I in no way felt that reading for a supporting role was beneath me. *It's okay*, I thought, *this will be a perfect* warm-up. *Get the juices flowing! This was actually GREAT. I could get a feel for the room before SHUTTING DOWN the competition with my Albert read.*

Mr. Sadowski called up Heather to read the role of Mrs. MacAfee opposite me. This was good. Heather was a drama club newcomer, so she was hungry and had a lot to prove. This was her moment too, and, as we locked eyes, I could tell she was ready to leave it all on the chorus room floor. LET'S FUCKING DO THIS.

The scene opens with Mr. MacAfee's entrance. He's furious. He's a fertilizer salesman who feels utterly invisible in his own life, and this is when he lets it all out. Now, a *lesser* actor would have come in screaming, but I knew I had to pace myself—start small, build, save the fireworks for the end. Everything Heather gave me was gold. She was the perfect doting wife trying to calm her husband down while, at the same time, saying the next thing to set him off. Her timing was impeccable—I made a mental note to tell her later that *I really saw something in her.* We were flying.

Looking ahead, I saw that my next line was to be delivered to the character's son, but nobody had been added to the scene to read that part. *This was it*, I thought. *My opportunity to take a risk, to do something big and memorable.* Still fully in character, I walked into the audience, right over to where my real-life neighbor Scott was sitting. Grabbing him by his *ear*, I pulled him out of his chair and delivered my line at top volume: "RANDOLPH, PUT THOSE CHEMICALS AWAY AND GO TO BED!"

The entire room exploded in laughter. I was killing it.

As I made my way back toward Heather, it hit me. This scene was going *too well.* I looked up at Mr. Sadowski. He was nodding and laughing, writing something down, showing it to another person. *No,* I thought. *Noooooo. This was my WARM-UP! My fun attempt to show that I was a good sport. WHY DID I HAVE TO BE SO GOOD AT EVERY-THING? WHY HAD I BEEN CURSED WITH SO MUCH TALENT?*

Mr. Sadowski asked most of the *The Way We Live Now* crew—Kate, Becca, Christian, and me—to stay after he released everyone from the audition. The cast list would be going up in the morning, but he wanted to tell us the good news in person. Jean-Luc, by the way, was not cast in the show. Mr. Sadowski had made it clear that it was Conrad or nothing, baby, and Jean-Luc chose nothing. He was a vaguely hot man of his word, I guess.

Mr. Sadowski pointed at each of us and called out the part we'd be playing. Christian would be Albert. Kate would be Kim, the MacAfee daughter. Becca would be Albert's overbearing mother. And I would be Mr. MacAfee, of course. I wasn't surprised. I hadn't even been given the opportunity to read for Albert. Was it because they wanted my sister to play his mother? THEY DON'T HAVE A KISSING SCENE, DO THEY?

Having been left with no other choice, I stood up and declared, "I QUIT." Then I turned and ran out of the room. The running was not added for dramatic effect. I literally ran out to the school parking lot and threw up. I know; sometimes my extra-ness knows no bounds.

. . . .

Yes, I truly believed that I deserved the lead role in my high school's spring musical. This entitlement didn't come from nowhere. I'd spent the previous summer at what I would tell everyone was an elite, pre-professional summer theater program: the Walnut Hill School for the Arts in Natick, Massachusetts. It was really more of a theater sleepaway camp for bored, weird, rich kids, but my jealous friends didn't need to know that.

Going to Walnut Hill was a really big deal for me. The six-week sleepaway program cost $4,000—more than my mother made in a month. But because she knew how important this was to me, God love her, she took out a bank loan to make it happen.

Over the course of the six weeks, the campers—er, *pre-professionals*—put on three small musicals and one big one. Sure, you could count on a part in the smaller musicals. But to be cast in the big musical, you had to audition against all the other kids in the program, and only the best of the best would be cast as leads. That year we were doing the Andrew Lloyd Webber rock opera *Evita*, a show about the Argentinian people and one woman's journey from illegitimate childhood to becoming the most powerful Latin American woman in history. A perfect choice for a bunch of sixteen-year-old white kids from New England.

The most intense part of the audition process was the literal "Evita-Off" that they held to determine who would play the title role. Having narrowed it down to three of the most talented campers—Maria, Julia, and Rachelle—the auditioners had each of the girls take a turn singing "Buenos Aires," a pop/rock song from the middle of Act One about the lengths Evita is willing to go to "make it."

And though I don't think the director intended that the entire camp gather and watch the Evita-Mania Smackdown that was about to take place, of course that's exactly what happened. The front wall of the rehearsal room was made entirely of glass, so the seventy or so other campers sat there and gawked as each of these girls belted out "Buenos Aires," transforming themselves from Massachusetts townies into the passionate, formidable María Eva Duarte de Perón. And let me tell you: These girls delivered. I mean, we're talking about a song that nearly wrecked the vocal cords of the great Patti LuPone. Not to mention the fact that the song, which is sung at about a hundred miles per hour, is a mix of English and Spanish lyrics and is packed with sexual innuendo that *might* not have been appropriate for a trio of brace-faced high school sophomores to try to out-sexualize each other with. And yet these girls, unclear as they *certainly were* about what any of the words meant, Were. Bringing. It. Sweat poured down their faces. Their necks were beet red, veins popping in their foreheads. It was a goddamn Evita Bloodbath.

Ultimately, the role went to Maria, who was for sure the most appropriate of the three, if for no other reason than she had brown hair. Julia was cast as "the Mistress," the only other female role in the show. And Rachelle went on to star in the *Twilight* movie franchise. It was a win-win-win for everyone.

Since I know the anticipation is absolutely killing you, I'll tell you that I was cast as Juan Perón, Evita's husband. From my limited research, the real Juan Perón was handsome, swarthy, and masculine. I, on the other hand, was chubby, pimply, and just out of the closet. So looking back, I have no idea how I landed one of the two leading male roles. Maybe they liked my tenor/alto range, since my voice had not fully changed yet. Or perhaps they were simply confident in the transformative power of the *brown-face they were going to make us all wear*? Who knows. At the time, none of this mattered to me. However it happened, I was now A Lead in the big musical of an *elite summer theater program*, just like I always imagined I'd be—a bona fide star. Finally, someone else was seeing it.

Not that the part would be a cakewalk. The first hurdle was Don Juan's actual attraction to women. I found this idea daunting, but a challenge I was up for? Question mark? Our director had made it clear to us that he wanted *real* sexual chemistry between our characters, even though we were just teenagers. There's a pivotal scene where Juan Perón and Evita first meet and, through the song "I'd Be Surprisingly Good for You," they quickly size each other up, realizing how mutually beneficial it could be to team up romantically. The scene is supposed to start out coyly and build to sexy. And I . . . was not getting it. Holding my prop champagne and fake cigarette, I was supposed to trail Maria around the stage "LIKE A STALKING CAT READY TO POUNCE!" the director would angrily shout as we ran the scene over and over again. It was not going well. I was coming off as less of a stalking tiger and more of a prancing pussycat.

What does it even mean to look like a "stalking cat ready to pounce"? Was that what sexual chemistry was? How was I supposed to know? What, exactly, was I supposed to draw on? I was a chubby gay virgin. I didn't know anything about sexual chemistry. Luckily, Maria offered to rehearse with me and try to get me to at least *act* like I knew what it was. We met under a tree by the pool on Walnut Hill's beautiful campus, and she tried to coach me into sexiness.

"Okay, this time, as I pass you, just look right at my butt," Maria directed.

"Got it." Looking at her butt as she passed, I wasn't yet feeling the sexual chemistry, but I wanted to be a good student.

"Great!" she said. "Let's run it again, and this time, it's all about my boobs."

"Right!" I'd definitely seen dudes stare at boobs before. This was so helpful. I was feeling straighter already.

As she shimmied past me, she suddenly stopped and gasped. "Oh my God!" she said, pointing in the direction of the pool. "Did you have any idea Logan was working with all that?"

Dear reader, if this were a film, this whole next sequence would be shot in slow motion. (Note to producers: the movie rights are *very* available.) Following Maria's pointed finger, I looked toward the pool where a boy named Logan was emerging, water pouring off his slick, wet figure.

And that's when all the straight left my body. Logan was a six-foot-tall god, with curly blond hair, blue eyes, and a perfectly chiseled face. And as my eyes drifted to his bare torso, something deep inside me physiologically shifted and I became a different person than who I was before. (I KNOW THAT'S A LOT. But this was a truly defining moment in my life, SO PLEASE LET ME HAVE IT.)

Let me explain. Do you know the movie actor Ryan Phillippe? You remember: the teen heartthrob from the '90s whose deal with the devil must be ironclad because, *oh my God*, how else is the nearly fifty-year-old keeping it so tight? First of all, Logan was the spitting image of Ryan Phillippe, so much so that he'd sometimes get mistaken for him on the street. But that's not the story I'm telling here. In 1999, Ryan Phillippe starred in the summer blockbuster *Cruel Intentions*, which is a movie about who cares because Ryan Phillippe shows his bare ass. Not to be crude, but this bare ass scene is so freaking hot, and so iconic, that it was THE sexual awakening for so many young gay people of my era. Ryan Phillippe himself said in an *Entertainment Weekly* interview that yes, he knew his butt made a lot of us gay.

My point is Ryan Phillippe's butt was to other gay men what Logan Hughes's bare torso was to me. I mean, I was already "out" in the *theoretical* way of being attracted to other guys, but it was that torso, in that moment, with all its muscly bumps and smooth, pale skin, that sealed the deal for me. Maria's butt and boobs, sexy as they absolutely were, were a ham sandwich to me. But Logan's torso . . . that torso was my sexual awakening. Sex. Sex was something I wanted to have. And I wanted it to be with him.

And then our eyes met. I gasped. Oh my God, how long had I been staring at him? I was horrified.

But then he smiled. And waved. I waved back.

That night, after lights-out, there was a knock at my bedroom door. When I opened it, there was Logan. Wearing just a pair of white boxer shorts with little red lips all over them. This was . . . a surprise. We'd known each other a little bit, but he mostly hung out with the group of five or six straight boys every theater camp has. And I hung out with the girls, the way nature intended. The closest we'd ever come to acknowledging each other was earlier at the pool when he waved to me while I was ogling him.

"Hi," he said. I could tell he was nervous. "Can I come in?"

"Yes!" I said, probably too quickly. It was after lights-out, and this camp had a very strict *stay the fuck in your room after lights-out* policy. I was a rule follower who lived in fear of getting in trouble. But whatever; this was worth the risk.

Now, I know what you're thinking: Gay sex stuff is about to happen! But no. Not yet. I sort of cherish this memory of my first ever *real* conversation with Logan because of how truly innocent and sweet it was. And yes, I also cherish it because he was basically naked. But this was not a Sex Rendezvous. Logan, and his incredible torso, had an honest-to-God question.

"How do you know that you're gay?" Logan asked, as he paced back and forth.

"Um . . . I don't know. I guess I've always known."

"Have you ever kissed a girl?" he asked.

"Yes. Once."

"Did you like it?"

"Um, well, I like her a lot. But no. Kissing her . . . no, I did not like that."

Logan thought for a while and continued to pace. I realized I'd never seen anyone actually *pace* before. This kid was definitely working some shit out. And then he said, "I like kissing girls."

"Good!" I said, genuinely happy that he was letting me in a little bit to whatever the hell was going on. I waited for what felt like an appropriate amount of time before asking, "Have you ever kissed a boy?"

"No," he said.

"Have you ever wanted to?" I asked. I hadn't suddenly discovered my inner gay stalking cat. This was not an invitation. I mean, it wasn't *not* an invitation, but I sort of knew that wasn't where the night was heading. Mostly, I just loved that Logan was having a conversation with me that he'd clearly never had with anyone else. We had a secret, kind of—a new, special bond.

He waited a minute before responding. "I don't know," he answered, sort of quizzically.

We stayed up for the rest of the night, just talking. Not about gay stuff, just about our lives, theater, and whatever else. I was utterly mesmerized by him, and I could tell that I was having an effect on him too. At some point, it became clear that we had to go to sleep. When he got up to leave, he said, "Can I give you a hug?"

"Yeah, of course," I said.

I wrapped my arms around him and pulled him in. And we just stood there in that embrace for a minute, feeling safe and warm. And then, because I was feeling silly and brave, I squeezed him and lifted him off the ground. He fell into me even more and it was heaven.

"I just wanted to take you off the planet for a second, give you a little break," I said.

"Thanks," he said. "That was perfect."

Anyway, if Juan Perón's story was ever going to be truthfully told on the stage, it wasn't going to be by me. As my summer of pre-professional acting training became more of a summer of secret late-night Logan hangouts, things did not get better at *Evita* rehearsals. Slowly, our exasperated director removed me from more and more scenes. The rousing Act Two opener when Evita sings "Don't Cry for Me Argentina" from the balcony of the home she shares with her husband? No Juan. Evita's deathbed moment? Juan was out of town. Her funeral? Juan apparently had other things to do. And so on, until our production of *Evita* was less about the exciting rise of a political leader and more about a neglected wife who just started running things because her husband was off . . . napping? Or something? I was maybe the only Juan Perón to have less than five lines.

· ·

But back at the *Bye Bye Birdie* auditions, my high school acting colleagues knew none of this. As far as they knew, I had been the star in my *elite summer acting program.* And now I was being asked to take a *supporting* role in my senior year spring musical! Who wouldn't quit the show and puke in the parking lot? Absolutely fucking not. Right? RIGHT? . . . Hello?

After two days of stewing and, like, not getting a call from Mr. Sadowski telling me that he'd rearranged all the parts to cast me as Albert and rectify his ridiculous mistake, I decided to be the bigger man. After school I marched into the chorus room and declared that I'd thought about it and that it would actually probably be good for me to not *always* be the lead and that this would be a good opportunity for me to try my hand at *character acting* and that I really believe that old saying that there are *no small parts* and can I please have my part back?

This was the right move. And you know what? I ended up crushing it as Mr. MacAfee. Maybe I'd never be a leading man, but I'd found my niche: as a hilarious side character standout.

But who even cared about acting anymore? For me, the best part of opening night was that Logan was coming. We'd seen a lot of each other during that school year. He'd spend the weekend with me on Cape Cod or I'd go up and spend the weekend with him in Boston, where he lived. Sometimes we'd even sleep in the same bed and fall asleep with our legs touching. And sometimes we'd sleep in separate beds, and I'd stay up all night hoping he'd change his mind and get in bed with me. One night he lay down on the floor next to my bed, and long after I thought he'd fallen asleep, he reached up, found my hand, and held it. We fell asleep that way, hand in hand.

But in all of that time, no actual sex stuff had ever happened. We'd talked about it a couple of times, but he wasn't ready and didn't know if he'd ever be. Plus, he'd been sort of dating this girl that he seemed to really like. But the night before opening night, he called me. "I want to be your first," he said. No "hello," no warm-up—just that.

"Um. Yes," I said nervously, knowing that I wouldn't sleep, eat, or maybe even breathe until after the show the next night.

Opening night went great. Christian was a very good Albert, and Heather, my audition partner, was hilarious as my wife, Mrs. MacAfee. Taking a page out of scene-stealer Kate's playbook, for the opening scene where the character simply answers a ringing phone, Heather placed herself on the opposite side of the stage from said phone and turned what should have been a nothing moment into a minutes-long monologue that went like this: *"Well, whoever could that be? Who would be calling so early in the day? Could it be Susan with that potpie recipe she keeps promising to give me? I'll never get through all of my chores with this constant interruption."* And of course, I was charming and brilliant as Mr. MacAfee.

Back at my house after the show, Logan and I said *very* quick goodnights to everyone and headed up to my room. I could tell that Logan was feeling very confident, but I was a wreck. Like, WHAT ON EARTH WERE WE ACTUALLY GOING TO DO NOW? What is sex? *What exactly was expected of my tongue?* I had solicited advice from my friend Stacy, who was a little more . . . experienced. What had she told me to do again?

And look, I'm not gonna get too graphic here, but I'll tell you this: When Logan leaned over and kissed me, the world stopped. Suddenly our hands were everywhere—that ripped torso was not to be believed—and then I realized to my horror that we had no music playing. Weren't you supposed to have some kind of soundtrack for your first time that you'd remember forever? *Think, Hinds, think!*

I ran over to my CD player. The options were few: either the Broadway cast recording of *Miss Saigon*, or *The Who's Tommy*, or one of . . . several . . . Indigo Girls albums. And before you judge me for this, I will have you know that knowing and loving these albums got me laid plenty in college. But *Tommy* wasn't right for this moment. *Miss Saigon* would require too much explanation. It HAD to be the Indigo Girls. It had to be their *Rites of Passage* album: so poetic and just so, so, so gay. I ripped open the jewel case, shoved the CD into the player, and skipped to the last song—"Cedar Tree"—a song about a man burying his wife? I guess, but who cares! We weren't going to be listening to lyrics, we just needed that sweet, sweet acoustic guitar and Amy and Emily's soft harmonies to set the mood.

I turned around to dive back in. And there was Logan lying on top of the covers, completely naked except for a pair of black Calvin Klein boxer briefs. My heart was pounding, but I was ready. It was time to make my blowjob debut.

As I was R.I.P.P.I.N.G. the boxer briefs off him, my friend Stacy's advice came back to me, just in time:

"It's all about speed," she had told me. *"You get that thing in your mouth and you bob up and down like your life depends on it."*

"What about teeth and stuff?" I asked.

"Don't worry about teeth," she said. *"They don't mind!"*

In retrospect, Stacy might have been less sexually experienced than I thought.

But there I was, living out the fantasy I'd had for over a year, following my friend's advice dutifully. And I realize now that this is a great example of how one can both succeed and fail at exactly the same time.

Mr. MacAfee might have been the peak of my acting career, but I definitely got better at blowjobs.

Chapter Three

MY DISASTROUS EVENING WITH BEA ARTHUR

I remember the exact moment that I knew I needed to let go of my acting dreams and pursue something—*anything*—else. I was a sophomore in college and my face was buried cheeks-deep in Tiffany Wagner's ass.

No, I wasn't giving heterosexual sex the good old college try. The exact opposite, in fact. I was doing the gayest thing possible: performing in the Emerson College spring production of *Gypsy*.

Now look, I'm not trying to start World War Gay over here, but I've never really understood why everyone *loooooooves* the musical *Gypsy*. And by "everyone," I mean the musical theater gays that make up about 98 percent of my social circle, so bear with me. I mean, the music isn't that great, the plot points all happen too quickly, *and* the show, "based on true events," leaves out the most interesting stuff.

The musical, which takes place in the 1920s, tells the story of Mama Rose, who pushes her children into show business on the vaudeville circuit. Sorta boring, right? Well in real life, after the showbiz thing, Rose moved to New York City, where she *opened a lesbian boarding house, took a lady lover, and then* shot her dead *when she came on to Rose's daughter.* And yes, gays-just-waiting-to-correct-me, I know that some of this is disputed, but still, I mean, where's *that* musical, Stephen Sondheim?

But even if it wasn't my personal favorite, I'd taken it as a great honor to be cast in the spring musical as a sophomore. That is, until I saw the cast list, which read, I swear to God:

```
Patrick Hinds . . . . . . . . Cow (back end)
```

This plum part comes at a point in the show when we see an actual musical scene from Mama Rose's vaudeville act that takes place on a farm and involves a dancing cow. I know you're already picturing how they accomplish the dancing cow bit: two people are completely covered in white drapery that's meant to look like the cow's body. The lucky actor cast as "Cow (front end)" gets the dignity of standing upright, whereas the person cast as "Cow (back end)," in this case *me*, has to bend over, hold Cow (front end) around the waist, and bury their face deep into Cow (front end)'s ass to serve as the cow's hind legs.

In addition to standing upright, Tiffany, as Cow (front end), also got the lines. Every thirty seconds or so, there's a break in the music where she would enthusiastically scream: "Moo Moo Moo Moo." As Cow (back end), I got to join her in the choreography. FUN! The little dance we did involved us hopping from side to side and then jumping and clicking our heels together—CUTE! It had taken me six weeks to learn the fifteen-second-long routine, but now here we were, the night of our final performance. The heel-clicking dance moment was upon us, and it was time to Bring. It. Home. But then, just as we leapt into the air, Tiffany let out a fart so deep and so thick that the word "pungent" doesn't fully capture it. And with my body bent over behind her to form the Cow (back end), this fart was launched Right. Into. My. Face.

Now look, people fart. I don't blame her for that. But this cow costume Dutch-ovenning was next level. The costume was completely enclosed, and so I was hot-boxed into convulsions. I coughed and wheezed, all while still trying to dance. I tried my best to stay bent over, but I had to let go of Tiffany's waist to wave my hands around underneath the costume to try to ventilate the area and just breathe. My eyes were watering from the odor, or was I just fucking crying?!

Cows are famously flatulent, but this was no Method acting. Through my tears I could see that Tiffany had stiffened from embarrassment and had fallen out of step. Suddenly, I panicked; she was the eyes of this operation—the only one of us who could see where we were headed—and she had to lead us to the foot of the stage for our little number. It was an eleven-foot drop from there into the orchestra pit, and even in our un-fartiest of times, we'd come dangerously close to toppling into it.

If I'm honest, Tiffany really didn't have the precision to be worthy of Cow (front end). She was just sort of wandering now, and her "Moo Moo Moos" were all over the place. I was certain that at any second we'd topple off the edge of the stage and fall to our deaths, crushing an innocent cellist beneath us who would groan, "Oh my God, *what* is that smell?" as the sweet relief of death took the three of us. What a way to close a show.

But then suddenly, thankfully, the number was over and we trotted off stage. Tiffany threw off the head of the costume and ran for, I'm guessing, the bathroom. I stood there in the wings, breathing deeply and finally accepting that the acting life was not for me. *Sweet Jesus, anything but this.*

· ·

But anything what? Without any real direction or idea of what I was going to do with my life now, I decided to spend the remaining two and a half years of my college life interning. They say internships are a great way to gain valuable work experience, but let's be honest here: This isn't entirely true. If you're like me and most of the people I went to college with, you're also doing these internships for college credits. Which you *pay for*. My college experience cost $30,000 per year. Per. Fucking. YEAR. In exchange, I got farted on, got the opportunity to pay someone to work for *them*, and got some, but not nearly enough, sex with bi-curious straight guys. (*Hi, Mike!*)

Anyway, I ended up interning on the *Matty in the Morning* show—Boston's number one morning drive radio show on Kiss 108 FM. If you're from anywhere near Boston, you know *Matty in the Morning*. Matt Siegel and his show are legendary; he is a famously contrarian host with his own unique takes on the news of the day. He was an institution in Boston who retired in 2022 after forty years on the air.

I'd been listening to the show since I was a kid, so I was very excited to get the gig. After all, famous people were on the show *all* the time, and now I was going to get to be a part of it! Whether it was watching in-studio acoustic concerts with Matchbox Twenty, hanging out in the green room with Tara Reid, or going on Red Bull runs

I suggested that I could run to a nearby subway station that had a Dunkin' Donuts to get the bagels for her. She thought this was a great idea but insisted on coming with me. So she took my arm and we walked to the train-station Dunkin' Donuts together. "We actually caused such a scene that they had to delay the Outbound Ashmont Red Line until we got our order," I said.

Then there was the time that I was sent to a film set to interview George Clooney. Never happened. And the time, at a Kiss 108 summer concert, that Alanis Morissette and I were talking backstage and Sarah McLachlan walked over to say hi. This actually did happen . . . to someone else. I heard him tell the story in the station break room after the concert. But it definitely *could* have happened to me.

The one time I came close to meeting an actual celebrity was when Melissa Etheridge came to town, and the radio team was going to her hotel suite for an interview. I mean, *Melissa Etheridge*, be still my pounding lesbian heart. But I was told I needed to stay back at the office to answer the phone. That one still hurts.

The point is: To my friends, I was the celebrity whisperer. Celebrities fucking loved me. Just ask J.Lo. So when it was announced that Bea Arthur would be coming to receive an award from Emerson's Musical Theater Society, Ellyn Marsh, my best friend and President of the Society, knew that I was the obvious choice to be Bea's host and guide for the weekend.

Bea. Arthur. Now, ladies and gays, please feel free to go make yourself a drink while I explain who Bea Arthur is to the one straight guy reading this book, probably to impress a woman. Hi, Derek!

Derek, Bea Arthur is a legend. She originated roles in *Mame* and *Fiddler on the Roof*. Those are classic American musicals, Derek. Musicals are basically movies, but they happen live on stage and there's singing. Bea Arthur even won a Tony Award (think Heisman Trophy, but for live theater) in 1966. She went on to star in groundbreaking TV shows like *All in the Family* (yes, the Archie Bunker one) and *Maude*, tackling important societal issues like abortion, homophobia, and racism. These were all way ahead of their time, but what we're really here to talk about is *The Golden Girls*.

On paper, *The Golden Girls* was just a sitcom about four older women who lived together in a house in Miami, who loved each other no matter what, and who saw each other through all of life's ups and downs. No, Derek, they didn't do a bunch of lesbian stuff on each other. But it *does* bring up a good question: Why do the gays love this show so much that it feels like our demand for it has almost single-handedly kept it on the air for nearly four decades? I think there are two reasons. First, thematically the show speaks directly to us because it's a show about "chosen family." It even had real gay characters—who were unapologetically out and living happy, full lives—pop in from time to time. This wasn't happening anywhere else on TV in those days. Am I losing you, Derek? I'm almost done. The second reason is the biting humor. Those ladies were savage, and none of them were more savage than Bea Arthur as Dorothy Zbornak.

Just a sample—Dorothy: "If I'd had the money, I could have been living in a swinging condo instead of with . . . I better not say anything till I've had my coffee." She takes a sip and continues. "A slut and a moron! . . . Sorry, it must be decaf." Dorothy had been through a lifetime of hurt, and her humor came from that pain. A lot of us relate to that. And she would cut a bitch with her tongue. Jesus, do we gays eat that up, Derek.

Okay, ladies and gays, get back in here, we're all caught up!

Bea was flying into Logan Airport on Friday evening, where I was to meet her and take her to her hotel. This was absolutely no sweat for a celebrity pro like me. I explained to Ellyn that it was basic celebrity protocol to greet Bea at the airport with a dozen long-stemmed roses and a stretch limousine.

She didn't bat an eye. "No problem, whatever you need."

I was going to make quite an impression.

At the time, my sister Becca was living in Boston, so I asked her to join me for the trip to the airport. We rode the T out to Logan together and found the terminal Bea would be arriving at. I walked right up to a security agent, three dozen roses in hand, and said, "We're here to meet a _celebrity_." I said the word "celebrity" slowly and discreetly, the way any top-notch celebrity fetcher would know to. I then asked the security guard if we could go wait at the gate for our _celebrity,_ and he said, "Sure, why not?" We didn't have a ticket for a flight, we weren't scanned, patted down, or checked in any way. We just walked down the ramp to the gate with our pile of roses. The pre-9/11 airport situation was wild like that—any old rose-wielding celebrity wrangler could just go wherever he wanted.

Bea's plane landed. From a distance, we heard sirens approaching. My sister and I ran to the window to see an ambulance screeching across the tarmac to meet Bea's plane.

"Oh my God," I said to my sister. "Bea's dead."

I'd been worried about this possibility for weeks. Any good gay can tell you that Bea Arthur was born on May 13, 1922. In Brooklyn. It was a Saturday. Which is to say that on that day at Logan Airport in 1999, she was 77. Meaning that to this college kid, she was oooooooold. Think about it: She was _seven_ when the Depression started. She was forty-one (!) the day Kennedy was shot. And to really drive it home for the gays, she was seventy-FUCKING-three on the day that Tonya Harding's husband hired that guy to kneecap our queen Nancy Kerrigan in Detroit. So to see her carted out of first class in a body bag on a stretcher would have been disappointing, but not really surprising.

Luckily, someone else must have had a medical emergency! Because a few minutes later, there was Bea Arthur walking through the door of the jet bridge into the terminal. I was so glad she was alive, but the feeling, it seemed, was not mutual. I could tell right away that she was in no fucking mood. And look: Cross-country airplane travel is tough on even the youngest and fittest of us. But by the looks of her, this had been a particularly rough journey. The internet tells me that she was five foot ten, but she loomed much larger in person. She was dressed head to toe in sweats and seemed to be wearing a powder-white wig that had twisted up on her at some point in the flight without her noticing. All in all, she looked a bit like a particularly pale and grumpy Andy Warhol on stilts after a very long night at Studio 54.

I was terrified, of course, but I was determined to ace my role as celebrity handler and not let my fear show. I walked right up to her and said, "Hi, Ms. Arthur. I'm Patrick from Emerson College's Musical Theater Society."

"Who the fuck are those for?" she asked, nodding toward my armful of roses.

"They're for you! It's such an honor to—"

"No they aren't," Bea interrupted. "I don't fucking want those—" and then I swear to God, she looked up and past me, as though she were waiting for the laughs from a phantom studio audience.

Now, Derek, I know you don't like Bea talking to me that way. Lord knows Jennifer Lopez never took that tone with me, for obvious reasons (I never met her). But I feel that I have to interrupt the story here to clarify that Bea Arthur was *famous* for her potty mouth. She *loved* telling people to fuck off, and people loved being told to fuck off by her. But "fuck" wasn't even her favorite four-letter word. A decade after our meeting, Rue McClanahan, who co-starred with Bea, Estelle Getty, and Betty White on *The Golden Girls*, would tell a story at Bea's memorial service: "When Bea met my husband, she shook his hand and said, 'Rue, I love. Betty White? . . . She's a fucking cunt.'" Bea Arthur apparently loved to use the C-word.

I wish I could say that Bea Arthur's sassy dressing-down somehow bonded us as gay icon and gay disciple—that I threw my limp wrist in the air, furiously snapping my fingers and saying things like "*GO OFF, BITCH,*" and "*YES MA'AM, YOU TELL A BITCH TO FUCK OFF WITH THOSE FUCKING FLOWERS,*" and that it was smooth sailing for the rest of the night. But that's not what happened. I instantly realized that I was in over my head and I stood there, speechless. I was no celebrity whisperer. I was a fraud.

"Let's get to baggage claim, Peter," Bea said to me. I saw my sister, whom Bea had yet to even acknowledge, open her mouth to correct Bea, and I shot her a glance that said *My name is Peter now and we will all learn to like it.* Bea stomped off as we trailed after her. Okay, so she hated the flowers and she didn't know my name. But I was sure she was gonna love the limo.

I was so relieved when I saw the car pulling up outside the terminal. It was just what I had ordered: a white stretch limousine long enough for twelve people, as long as a school bus, with tinted windows. Very sleek. The driver was having a bit of trouble navigating something that large through the chaos of an international arrivals pick-up zone. Because this was Boston, what had started out as some mild horn honking quickly escalated into grown men and women leaning out their windows, flipping birds, and screaming at the limo driver:

"Get the fahk outta the way!"

"Fig-ya out how to fahkin pahk that fahkin boat!"

"Move, ya fahkin loosah befowah I pahk it up yoah ass!"

Bea was . . . not impressed.

"That car is not for us, Peter," she stated. This was not a question.

"It is!" I said cheerfully, fully considering stepping in front of the oncoming Avis shuttle bus.

"You've got to be fucking shitting me," Bea said.

Once inside the limo, things only got worse. The roof was lined with strips of neon-colored lights, alternating green, blue, and pink in a pattern for the full length of the ceiling like a 1980s nightclub. And since there were only three of us in a car built for twelve, there was a lot of open seating. My instinct was to sit as far away from Bea as possible, but that felt impossibly rude, as if manners were suddenly important. Honestly, part of me feels that Bea might have liked me more if I'd *been* impossibly rude. What would have happened if I went to the opposite end of the car and yelled, "I'll be down here if you need me, you miserable old witch! AND FIX YOUR FUCKING WIG, CRONE!"? It would either be my life's biggest mistake or its greatest triumph. But I was too scared. Instead, I sat close to her, determined to make some kind of connection.

The Tony-winning actress Donna Murphy was being honored along with Bea the following night, so I said, "What an honor to have both you and Ms. Murphy in the same room tomorrow night!"

"If I'd known she was coming, I wouldn't have made the trip," she responded. "Is there a bar in this thing?" she added, squinting down the expanse of the limo's interior.

"No," I said meekly, knowing it was the wrong answer. And then, because I'm a glutton for punishment, I added, "We asked them to take it out."

"That was the *wrong* decision, Peter."

Yes, Bea. Yes, it was.

We rode most of the way into Boston in awkward silence, under the relentlessly cheerful disco lights. As we drove through Kenmore Square, Bea finally piped up: "I'm hungry. Is there a place to stop for a meal?"

It was after 10 PM, and the only place I knew that would be open in the area was Pizzeria Uno. Not exactly an A-List establishment, but maybe Bea was big on Chicago-style deep-dish pizza.

"I don't know if you're a fan of Chicago-style deep dish—"

"Do they have a bar?" Bea asked.

"Surely," I said, using that word for the first time ever.

"Great, let's go there."

The limo pulled up right in front of Uno's. I got out, then my sister Becca. Then the two of us set to hoisting the nearly six-foot-tall, seventy-seven-year-old, grumpy-ass drag queen of a woman out of the car. It's not easy to delicately extract a gigantic, but fragile, elderly lady from a stretch limo. We grasped and pulled at her, we heaved and hoed, as she swatted us off and finally allowed us to yank her out. This wasn't the sort of celebrity handling I'd had in mind. Eventually we had her standing upright, now with her wig only slightly more askew.

Bea strode off into the restaurant and we scrambled after her. Before she even sat down, she took the hostess's arm and said, "I'll have a double Absolut Citron, neat." That's basically just four ounces of warm vodka in a glass.

We were seated right away, and once her drink arrived, the mere presence of it seemed to mellow her a bit. Looking back, I don't know why I didn't order four ounces of warm vodka for myself and just get hammered with her. I didn't drink much then, but as a . . . more than casual drinker now, I can see how that might have softened things a little. Like, maybe, *maybe*, if I had loosened up and cracked a joke about how I had no idea what I was doing—that I'd lied my way into this handler gig—and that I was terrified and that I JUST WANTED HER TO LIKE ME, she might have let me in. As I've learned in many a fraught moment since, authenticity and vulnerability usually go a long way. And who knows where the night might have taken us? Imagine if I'd rolled up into Jacques, the famous gay piano bar around the corner, with a hammered Bea Arthur! I could've been the gay toast of the town. But instead, I ordered a Diet Coke and girded myself for more abuse.

"Peter," Bea said, addressing me, aka Patrick. "I'd like to discuss my itinerary for tomorrow." She reached into her bag and pulled out a schedule that had been sent to her by Douglass, Ellyn's number two at the Musical Theater Society.

She then went into a lengthy explanation of what exactly was *totally wrong* about the plans he had made for her. Douglass had scheduled Bea for a blowout at a salon on Newbury Street at 5:30 PM. A car would pick her up from there at 7:30 PM to take her directly to the theater and the reception afterwards. Bea hated this: "That's way too much time at the salon!"

I didn't know much about blowouts at the time, but I imagined it had to do with, like, blow-drying hair? So this confused me because Bea, as had been established the moment I met her, was wearing a wig . . . right? Instantly, because my brain is constantly cycling through an incredibly gay Rolodex of celebrity anecdotes, I thought about the time I saw Dolly Parton on *Oprah*. An audience member asked her how long it took to do her hair. Dolly famously answered, "How would I know? I'm never there!"

The question was: How could I possibly ask this mean old lady if we were dealing with a Dolly Parton situation here? Because if so, couldn't someone just, like, pick up her hair from her at the hotel, take it to the salon to have it styled and then just meet her at the theater with it or whatever? (The absolute glamour of it all.)

I eyed Bea. She eyed me right back. I didn't think I could ask about the wig without getting her now empty vodka glass thrown at my head. I longed for the days of walking arm in arm into a subway-station Dunkin' Donuts with Gwyneth Paltrow. Those were(n't) the days. But Bea had me scared to death, and this wig stuff was out of my league.

"Let me go call Douglass," I said.

Douglass was never my favorite. He was tall and skinny and good-looking, I guess. He was effeminate—which was adorable, but he was also deeply closeted, which was annoying—especially since everybody knew that he'd bottomed for just about every gay and gay-curious guy at Emerson. (I'll explain bottoming to you later, Derek.) I called Douglass from the pay phone at the back of the restaurant.

"Yo," Douglass said, answering the phone, trying, but failing, to place the word in a low register. Eye roll. I explained the situation to him, but he said that the salon had made the schedule based on how long they thought it would take. Great, fine, this explanation seemed reasonable enough to take back to Bea.

When I got back to the table, my sister and Bea were laughing like old friends. *Amazing*, I thought. *We've turned a corner.* But then Bea saw me, and her smile evaporated.

"Did you talk to Douglass?" she asked, getting his name right on the first try.

"I did," I said, cheerily. "It was actually the salon that determined the timetable based on their expert opinion of what you wanted to have done."

Bea stared at me. Then she pounded the table with both fists. "WELL THEN CLEARLY YOU DIDN'T TALK TO DOUGLASS!" she shouted.

We ate our food quickly and then piled back into the limo to bring Bea to the Ritz-Carlton, where Emerson had sprung for a huge one-bedroom suite facing the Boston Common. Did I mention that it took me almost twenty years to pay off my student loans?

She waved off the bellhop. "No, no. You take the bags, Peter. And then get me on the phone with Douglass."

At this point, I was too exhausted to argue. Once I'd hauled her bags up to her room, I dialed Douglass's number and handed her the phone.

"'Yo?'" she said. "What kind of decent person answers the phone like that? Look, Douglass, it's Bea. I'm sorry to be such a cunt, but we really need to straighten out the salon timing for tomorrow . . . uh-huh. Okay. Perfect."

She hung up the phone. "Douglass said he'd take care of it first thing tomorrow, Peter. Honestly, I don't know why you were being so difficult about it. At least *Douglass* understands!"

I was at the end of my rope and ready to wrap up this particular celebrity encounter. "Great. Anything else you need before I go?" I asked.

"Yes," Bea said. "Find me on TV. I like to fall asleep to the sound of my own voice."

And I swear to God, at that moment I knew I'd put this in a book someday. I flipped through the channels and, of course, it didn't take long to find an episode of *The Golden Girls*. I put down the remote and headed for the door.

"Good night," I said.

"Toodaloo," she responded, settling in to sleep in front of her own, frankly iconic, Emmy-winning performance.

I gently closed the door behind me, hoping that the next time I saw Bea Arthur, she'd be berating Rose, Blanche, and Sophia instead of me.

. . . .

A few years later, I actually did see her again in person. I had moved to New York and was bartending at a restaurant when Bea walked in. Her one-woman show *Just Between Friends* had just opened on Broadway. She was pushing eighty years old and still doing the damn thing. Gotta love her.

When she walked into the bar, our eyes met. I, of course, had zero expectation that she would remember me, but her face lit up and she walked directly over. She took my hands and said, "We meet again!" It was such a sweet, kind thing to say, and she truly seemed happy to see me. "Can you join us for a drink?"

"I'd love to," I said.

I grabbed the biggest highball glass I could find and filled it to the top with warm citron vodka. I brought it to her table where she introduced me to her young male companion.

"This is Patrick," she said, indicating the *other* guy at the table. "He's my friend and longtime makeup artist."

I extended my hand to him and said, "Hi, I'm Peter."

"That's right," Bea said. "Peter and I shared a lovely weekend in Boston a few years ago."

The three of us had a wonderful chat for about thirty minutes. Before I excused myself to close up the bar, Bea said, "I'd love for you to be my guest at the show sometime in the next few weeks. Come backstage after and then we'll go out for dinner."

"Sure, I'd love to," I said, knowing I'd never take her up on it. And I never did, which I think I regret now. If I had been guaranteed the cheerful and friendly Bea I'd met in the bar that night, I would have done it. And maybe this time I *would* have had that warm double shot with her. But for me it was better not to gamble. *Let this moment be the end to the story when I write the book someday, it's such a good one.*

"Good night, Peter. And thank you," Bea said, raising the now empty glass of vodka that I'd brought her.

"Good night, Bea," I said. "And thank YOU."

Chapter Four

ON NOT MAKING IT IN NEW YORK

For my senior year of college, I left my internship at the *Matty in the Morning* show and got a new internship at the NBC TV affiliate in Boston, working in the newsroom and on a Sunday morning show. It was fast-paced, hectic, and exhausting—and I fucking loved it. In January of that year, when I started thinking about what I'd do after graduation, someone suggested that I apply for the NBC page program in New York City.

In the world of television, the NBC page program is a bit legendary—and became even more so after it was immortalized by Jack McBrayer's character Kenneth on *30 Rock*. The program is basically a chance for recent college graduates with dreams of working in television to get a foot in the door with a major TV network. It's not glamorous work; you mostly do low-level audience services jobs on shows like

Saturday Night Live and *The Tonight Show* in exchange for something like fifteen dollars an hour. Not exactly a "living wage" for Manhattan, but who cares? THAT'S WHAT CREDIT CARDS ARE FOR!

In doing the required eleven minutes' worth of research for this chapter, I just learned a bunch of stuff that I'm very glad I didn't know going into the application process. According to the NBC page program's Wikipedia entry, which is a thing that apparently exists, *"Selection is highly competitive, with only 212 pages selected each year out of more than 16,000 applicants."* Like, WHAT? Doing the math, that means that their acceptance rate is only about 1.5 percent. As Wikipedia points out, *"becoming an NBC page is more competitive than gaining admission to Ivy League universities."* Settle the fuck down, NBC; these geniuses are literally pointing people to bathrooms and, like, herding tourists into elevators. Curing AIDS, it is not.

But I didn't know any of that until, well, five minutes ago. So, after I applied to the page program and was invited to a group interview in New York, my biggest problem was how? I was not a person of means in college. In addition to my NBC affiliate internship and full class load, I was working twenty hours a week at a local coffee shop for spending money and all the bagel sandwiches I could eat. How was I going to get to the interview? I wasn't making Amtrak money and a hotel room in the Big Apple for the night was . . . outside of my budget.

My bright idea was to take a 2:30 AM bus from Boston to New York. That meant getting into New York a little after 7 AM—plenty of time to find a public bathroom to splash some water on my face and get to 30 Rockefeller Plaza for my 9 AM group interview. And lest you think I was made of money, this was not some kind of fancy forty-dollars-each-way Greyhound bus. No. I decided to take advantage of the Chinatown bus. Yup, for only ten dollars, I could hop on a bus in Boston's Chinatown and a little over four hours later hop off that same bus in Chinatown, New York City. And yes, that is a pretty sweet deal. I mean, did the buses always have heat, air conditioning, and/or functioning bathrooms? Absolutely not. Did the drivers regularly obey speed limits, traffic rules, and just general commonsense safety measures? That's a hard "no." Was I once on one of the buses when the engine caught fire and filled the entire cabin with smoke, forcing the driver to cross four lanes of traffic at top speed in order to pull into a rest area and strand all of us passengers for several hours? Yes, yes I was. Did that deter me from taking the bus again in the future? Not in the slightest.

Luckily, this time I did not burn to death on the highway. I made it safely enough to New York and met up with the other job candidates in the lobby at 30 Rock. Looking around, it was clear that these kids had done their research on whatever the year 2000 equivalent of Wikipedia was (*Ask Jeeves?*), because they were Ready™, with their briefcases and pressed suits—and, I'M SORRY, BUT AREN'T WE APPLYING TO CHANGE TOILET PAPER ROLLS IN TOURIST BATHROOMS? OR ARE WE SITTING FOR THE FUCKING BAR EXAM? Anyway, in contrast, my suit was five-hours-on-a-bus wrinkled, and the clasp for my clip-on tie—yes, clip-on—had snapped. Now there was a hole where the "knot" was supposed to be.

These kids looked rested and prepared. I looked exhausted and rumpled. But I didn't care because I had *a plan*. Janel, one of the producers I worked with at the TV station in Boston, had been a page many years before and had given me the inside scoop.

"There will be eight or ten of you in the interview," she said. "So, when they ask a question, you want to be the first one to answer—show them you're eager, a go-getter."

"What kinds of questions?" I asked.

"They'll be vague, but they'll give you an opportunity to tell them something about yourself—something that makes you unique or different. Remember, diversity is important!"

I nodded my head knowingly. There it was. The magic word. *Diversity.* I mean, I was gay; that counted, right? And I mean, not just gay, but like GAAAAAAAAY! I sounded gay, I laughed pretty gay, I even walked with a little bit of a swish. I could get even swishier if need be. I was very gay! Ugh, finally, this gay thing was going to pay off for me!

Also, the timing of my interview was perfect because NBC was at its very gayest. They were two years into their smash-hit super gay sitcom *Will & Grace*. And that fucking peacock logo was basically a Pride flag. If I could find a way to make sure my gayness was front and center, I'd be golden.

As our interviewer, who bore a shocking resemblance to Salma Hayek, led us into the conference room for the interview, I muttered a mantra to myself. It was a cheat sheet I'd created to remind myself how to nail this thing: *Be first, be gay, be very very gay. Be first, be gay, be very very gay.*

Salma Hayek showed us to our seats, welcomed us, and then dove right into the first question: "I'd like each of you—"

My hand shot straight into the air. *BE FIRST, BE GAY, BE VERY VERY GAY* was pounding in my head like a goddamn battle cry.

"Oh," Salma Hayek said, a little bit startled. "Um, I'll just finish the question and then you can go first if you'd like."

"That would be great," I said confidently, and a little gayly.

"So . . . you can go ahead and put your hand down."

"Oh! Ha!" I said, and then followed her instruction.

She continued: "I'd like each of you to tell me about a time when you faced adversity and were able to overcome it."

Oh my God, I thought. *OH MY GOD. It was too good to be true. ADVERSITY and DIVERSITY in the same question? I scanned the room. These poor suckers, with their real ties and faces so well rested from "being able to afford a hotel room before the big interview." What sort of adversity had these idiots ever known?*

"Mr. Hinds, you can go now if you want," Salma said.

"Yes, thank you," I said. *BE FIRST, BE GAY, BE VERY, VERY GAY . . . AND POOR!* I quickly amended my mantra to take full advantage of the moment.

"I grew up very poor," I continued. "I'm the second of four kids and my mom worked a lot, so I also didn't get a lot of parenting."

Wait, what . . . WHAT? This was off script, and not even really true? Or wait—WAS IT? Suddenly my heart was pounding. I had no idea what I was saying. Why had I changed my mantra at the last minute? Stupid! Stupid! My brain went into gay drama club overdrive: *INTRODUCE A PROP! INTRODUCE A PROP TO DISTRACT, YOU FUCKING IDIOT!*

I pulled off my dangling clip-on tie and held it up. "I mean, look at me; I'm almost twenty years old and I still don't know how to tie a tie."

Someone chuckled. I panicked.

"I also didn't have a dad because my mom is gay."

Salma Hayek jumped in: "Okay, thank you Mr. Hin—"

"NO!" I yelled. Everyone in the room jumped. "Wait! No, I meant that I'M gay! Not my mom. No, well my mom is gay too, but that's not the story I was telling!"

"Thank you, Mr. Hinds. We really need to move on," Salma said.

"Okay!" I said. And then all at once: "I was just trying to say that I was poor and gay—very gay—and high school was . . . adverse! . . . but then I came out and learned to be myself! And then I met a boy at an elite summer theater program, and he sort of became my boyfriend."

I was off the rails. The room fell silent. Salma Hayek stared at me, eyes wide and mouth gaping. Oh my God. Was she worried about me?

"Anything else, Mr. Hinds?" she asked.

"Diversity is . . . good."

So no, I was not accepted into the Ivy League of Fetching Coffee for Late-Night Talk Show Hosts.

. . . .

Back in Boston a week later, my producer Janel came to me with another opportunity. CNBC, the financial news sister network of NBC, was hiring a news associate for one of their daily live shows, *Power Lunch*. A news associate, Janel explained, is basically an assistant to the production team. "You help the editors cut tape for the show and you get to be in the control room during the show each day. You should go for it."

It sounded interesting . . . enough. And if I got the job, it would be a foot in the door with the company I thought I wanted to work for. So, I applied, quickly got an interview and bada-bing, bada-boom, I got the job! As exciting as that was, it's possible that there weren't a *ton* of applicants for this position. First of all, *The Tonight Show* this was not. *Power Lunch* was a daily financial news show that "delves into the economy, markets, real estate, media, and technology." Exciting, no? Matt Damon wasn't exactly dropping by *Power Lunch* that often. Second, the CNBC studios were not located in the iconic and impressive landmark 30 Rock building in Rockefeller Center, New York City.

They were located on the other side of the Hudson River in the not iconic, nor impressive Fort Lee, New Jersey. The nearest landmark was the Quiznos in the strip mall across the street. You know, the one next to the UPS Store. But who was I to be picky? I might be some kind of bootleg CNBC Kenneth, but I still felt lucky to have a "real job" to go to after graduation. I was on my way . . .

. . . to New Jersey, it turned out. My friends Tyler, Sarah, Laurie, and I were all headed to the New York area after graduation, so we decided to find a place together. The cheapest, most convenient location seemed to be Jersey City. It was less than a mile from Manhattan, and we were told that there was an easy subway—the PATH train—that got you into the city in less than fifteen minutes. Perfect, right? Not exactly.

And this is where we need to take a slight detour and discuss a failure of a different kind that has haunted me since my days of living in New Jersey. Don't worry, we'll get right back to embarrassing stories about me, because how could ME working at a conservative FINANCIAL NEWS NETWORK not end in a hellfire of humiliation. I promise, it does. But before we get there, we gotta talk about the laissez-faire attitude the people of New Jersey have toward getting in cars with strangers.

Here's the thing: My roommates and I lived about a MILE from that "very convenient" PATH train, so we relied on shuttle buses on the main avenue to take us back and forth from our part of town. Fine. But after 10 PM, *the shuttle buses stop running*. So, in that pre-Uber and Lyft era, this resulted in a makeshift and, to my knowledge, unregulated situation with random "taxi drivers" picking people up at the station on the New Jersey side, asking their destination, making up the cost of the ride, and then driving them to wherever they were going. In their personal cars. This was just accepted practice, as I learned late one Saturday night when I made my way to the spot where the shuttle bus normally stopped only to find a line of, like, Toyota Corollas. The guy in the car at the front of the line saw my confusion and said, "Get in or walk." All around me, I watched other people get into the regular cars of total strangers. Somehow, *I* was being the weirdo by not putting myself in an obvious true crime situation. So, I gave in and plopped down in the back seat, where I found a baby sound asleep in a car seat next to me. I gave the driver my address. "Seven dollars plus tip," he said, and off we went.

And this isn't the only place in New Jersey where I've seen something like this! On the New Jersey side of the George Washington Bridge—the bridge connecting New Jersey and Manhattan—there is a place where people stand on the *side of the highway* to be picked up by solo drivers who want to get the carpool discount on the bridge toll and save *five dollars*. Reminder: You are both complete fucking strangers to each other. Are you aware that, according to some reputable sources who track these things, there are something like 2,100 active serial killers on the prowl in the US at any given time? New Jerseyans: Is it worth FIVE DOLLARS to end up on my podcast?

Anyway, the location of our apartment was ideal for commuting into Manhattan most of the time. But it was not ideal for commuting to Fort Lee. The PATH train was not designed to move people from New Jersey suburb to New Jersey suburb, so my commute was a long and winding ninety minutes, requiring multiple transfers. Which, of course, I didn't find out until the morning of my first day of work because it had never, not once, occurred to me that I should give it a dry run.

And that's why I was late on my first day. Not a good look. When the bus finally came to a halt in front of the CNBC building, I sprinted inside and onto the elevator. A small, well-dressed woman walked in after me. Remember that scene in *The Devil Wears Prada* where the person flees the elevator that they were in first so Meryl Streep can have it all to herself? And they apologize to her on the way out? This woman was bringing that big Meryl Streep energy, but I just stood there panting like a doofus. I was late and had just sprinted twenty whole feet.

I'd find out later that she was none other than THE Maria Bartiromo—CNBC's big STAR—the person who made *Power Lunch*'s Bill Griffeth look like, well, Bill Griffeth. She was no one to me, but because she had made it big in this "man's world" of television finance, she was better known at the time by a demeaning and downright stupid nickname: "the Money Honey." Barf, barf, barf.

And I gotta tell you, this broad was in no mood that morning to be sharing an elevator with a nervous, sweaty queen-boy who didn't know enough to vacate the elevator at the mere sight of her. The situation did not improve fifteen seconds later when the elevator slowed between floors, literally bounced, and then stopped. Now, I have a truly serious fear of being stuck in an elevator. And I'm guessing maybe the Money Honey does too because she *wheeled* around—in like eight-inch stilettos—and glared at me as though I had, somehow, orchestrated this. *THIS NEVER HAPPENS WHEN I TRAVEL ALONE*, her dark and narrowed eyes screamed at me. And I can only imagine what my face was serving in return; I was terrified for being stuck, terrified for being late, and now I was terrified that this gorgeous angry raccoon-woman, her eyes lined and shadowed for days, was going to maul me to death right then and there.

"You're not gonna freak out, are you?" she hissed. The Money Honey did not mince words.

I just shook my head. She squinted. My timidity seemed to enrage her even more, and her mouth curled into a sneer of contempt. I could see tomorrow's headline:

SWEATY GAY IDIOT MURDERED BY MONEY HONEY

But then, poof, the elevator started moving again and her face became beautiful once more. When the doors opened, she vanished into a sea of cubicles, and I stood there, shaken, but grateful to be alive. It was 9:17 AM.

. . . .

It would become quickly, and I think mutually, clear that I was not a good fit for the CNBC job. I should state plainly that it was absolutely *not* because I was a raging homosexual in a fairly conservative workplace. I mean, I'm sure my general *excitement* and high-pitched squawking didn't *help*—sorry for being awesome and fun!—but no, it definitely wasn't that. I just wasn't *invested* . . . which is an unfortunate and unintended financial pun, so I guess the curse of being exceptional at everything rages on.

During my interview process, I had been very clear that I didn't know anything about finance, just in case my broken clip-on tie and rumpled suit hadn't clued them in. I didn't oversell myself as someone who understood "the markets" or investing or even as someone who had a checking account. I did, however, over-promise my eagerness to get up to speed quickly—I'd vowed to read the *Wall Street Journal* every night and maybe even take an evening economics class so I could learn to, you know, speak the language!

Obviously, I did none of these things. And at work, I wowed no one with my work ethic. I maybe wasn't even CNBC Kenneth-level. This became clear one Monday morning about a month into the job, when Michael, one of the edit guys, called me over to his desk. A friend of his from a news station in South Africa had sent him raw footage of a surfer being attacked by a great white shark. "Check it out," he said. "She lost an arm, but she kicked the living shit out of the thing right there in the open ocean!"

Real-life shark gore isn't really my thing, but then again neither was the S&P 500. We sat there watching that fifteen-minute tape over and over, reveling in this lady-badassery as she punched and kicked her way out of this shark's mouth. We were mid–high five for the third time when Rachel, the executive producer of my show, found us. When I had first met Rachel, I learned that earlier in her career she had worked on the TV show *ALF*. Freaking *ALF*—the iconic '80s sitcom about the lovable cat-eating alien! You'd think that someone who worked on *ALF* would be fun, but you'd be very, very wrong. And honestly, her journey from making fun-loving alien puppet TV on a sunny Hollywood back lot to making dry, puppet-free financial news TV in a gloomy New Jersey suburb is probably a fall from grace too epic to dwell upon. If I were her, I guess I'd be a grump too.

"PATRICK!" she screamed. She wasn't really a yeller, but boy oh boy did I bring that out in her. "Where have you been? You missed the morning meeting and we're fifteen minutes to air and OH MY GOD WHAT THE HELL ARE YOU GUYS WATCHING?"

Michael had paused the video at the moment just after the shark had bitten through this poor woman's arm. There was blood and flesh and bone everywhere. Michael and I just stared at Rachel.

"Oh, you've got to be FUCKING KIDDING ME," she screamed as she stormed off down the hallway.

I never even got to tell her that the woman *lived*.

Now, I'm not saying the producers of the show began a campaign to get rid of me soon thereafter, but that's what it felt like. The following week, Rachel told me that she was sending me and our intern Sabrina out of the office to do a story on Macy's new fall fashion line. We'd be going to the flagship store in Herald Square in Manhattan to shoot B-roll. And then Sabrina and I would be modeling (?!) some of the clothes.

Maybe she was just trying to get me out of her hair for the day. Or maybe she thought I'd relish the opportunity to be on camera? And it's not like CNBC was going to spring for real models. But, come on, why on earth would Rachel want *me* to do it, other than because it would be embarrassing for me and hilarious to her. See, Rachel: that's the kind of fun-loving sense of humor your *ALF* friends probably used to love about you!

When Sabrina, the camera crew, and I got to the store, a cheery PR woman met us at the back entrance. "Thanks for coming," she said. "This is very exciting for us! Do you know when the models are getting here?"

My stomach dropped. *Oh my God*, I thought. *Rachel didn't tell her.* Somewhere in East Asshole, New Jersey, Rachel was probably doubled over in laughter, thinking about this very moment. I had to respect the game. Good one, Rachel. Good one.

"You'rrrrrre looking at 'em!" I said, trying to sound confident.

The PR lady froze. I could tell she didn't want to be rude, but she was also very much trying to figure out if I was joking. Nobody spoke. Her clenched smile faded. Finally, she cocked her head and took a look at Sabrina. Sabrina was eighteen, brunette, and *perfectly fine looking*. She seemed to pass the test. Then the PR lady looked at me and—I know you're expecting me to say something hilariously self-deprecating, but you know what? I was fucking fine looking too! Yes, I was a little round in the middle, and *sure* my face had the jaw-line of a puffer fish, but I was a solid "6" who came from a long line of "5s," and goddammit, I was making it work.

"Well," the PR lady said. "We'll just have to see what we have in your size."

When the crew was done shooting their B-roll footage, it was time for the dreaded fashion show. A whole section of the men's department had been cordoned off, lit, and staged for the shoot, with the aisle decked out like a runway. This shit was professional.

Sabrina went first and really rose to the occasion; she was a natural! They had done her hair and makeup and she looked very sexy and confident in her earth-toned pantsuit with an open mid-length coat.

My clothes weren't as sexy. Having dressed me in a pair of loose brown corduroys; a generic blue button-down shirt; and boxy gray sports coat, it seemed like they were just trying to hide my body under as many layers as possible. The stylist kept buttoning and unbuttoning the sports coat, trying to determine which was less bad. Eventually, she gave up.

And look—terrified and awkward as I was feeling, I knew there was only one way to do this: I had to leave it all on the runway, like the former capital-E *Elite* summer theater program alum that I was. I had to go all in.

It was just like back in seventh-grade English class, when I'd done a presentation on *Go Ask Alice*. You know: the classic young adult book about a fifteen-year-old girl who develops a drug addiction, gets clean, and ultimately relapses and dies. To really make a splash with my presentation, I made a short video where I dressed in full costume *as* Alice—we're talking white blouse, blue tie-dye miniskirt borrowed from my sister, and . . . a shoulder-length BLONDE wig. While the video played in the classroom, I ran down the hallway to change into the costume so that I could reappear, *in character*, at the video's conclusion to make a "just say no to drugs"–inspired speech to my class. As I was wrestling myself into the miniskirt in the public middle school bathroom, I had a sudden jolt of fear.

Oh shit, had I miscalculated?

Was full drag maybe not the *best* option for an awkward, effeminate thirteen-year-old who just hoped to get through the day without getting punched in the face in the hallway during a passing period?

I started to panic.

The miniskirt suddenly felt *very very* mini.

But then I stood up straight, adjusted my wig, and thought, *Fuck that, I have a monologue about the dangers of recreational gateway drug use to deliver, and I'm gonna do it looking like Miss Piggy stuffed into a sausage casing because that was the only way to make them* really *hear me*. I had to do it for *them*. I kicked the bathroom door open and strutted down the hallway back to class.

Confidence was key. Confidence would sell the outfit. Confidence would keep me from getting sucker punched between classes. I mean, it wouldn't, but a seventh-grade drag queen can dream.

I did my best to bring this same energy to the shitty Macy's runway. I clomped and strutted and then, thankfully, the whole thing was over. That is, until the next day when the segment aired live at the top of the show. The director, a hot Jersey guy named Andy, called for the segment to be played, and I desperately hoped that everyone would take a break from the usually fast-paced live show and run to the bathroom, grab a coffee, or really do anything else but watch my fashion show. But when Hot Andy exclaimed, "Oh my God!" everyone stopped and stared at the monitor, where Model Me was striding toward the camera.

I remember the producer telling me to look serious and "intentional." INTENTIONAL??? What kind of direction was that? Instead, I looked like I was trying to make a "sexy model face." With my pursed lips and furrowed brow, I looked like an old person scowling while trying to read some fine print on a medicine bottle. But that wasn't even the worst of it. The camera angle was so low that it made my entire shape look rounder than it was. And my face! My *FACE*! So pale! So . . . moon shaped! So utterly lacking in any spatial differentiation between my chin and my neck. What kind of swamp-dwelling, neck-less sea creatures did I come from?? How had no one in my entire genetic lineage ever even once found a person with a jawline or fucking cheekbones to procreate with??(!!!)?

Everyone in the control room stared at the screens, their mouths hanging open. Back on the runway, Model Me turned and walked away from the camera, my shapeless blob of a body looking huge in those oversized clothes. And then I stopped.

Oh shit. I'd forgotten about this part.

With my back to the camera, Model Me slowly removed the sports coat, hung it on my thumb, and flung it over my shoulder. Then I swiveled from the waist up, turning back toward the camera, looked directly into it, and *smoldered*.

That was it; my colleagues in the control room couldn't keep it together any longer. Their laughter was . . . unbridled. And then Hot Andy said, "I'm sorry man, but we're taking that again in slow motion as we go into the break." Which he did. As Slow-Mo Model Me smoldered for all the at-home audience to see, Producer Rachel laughed so hard she had to put her head down on the table in front of her.

. . . .

After becoming the laughingstock of *Power Lunch*, it's fair to say that I was losing my focus at work. Instead of rising through the ranks of boring, shitty CNBC to the upper echelons of the glamorous, iconic, gay heaven of NBC, it seemed increasingly clear that my days were numbered.

So, it was no surprise when I started fucking up even more than I had previously. A few days after my fashion show, we were covering "breaking news" about a company whose "stock" had "fallen sharply" overnight—whatever any of that means. We were twenty minutes into the two-hour show, which was live, mind you, and somehow watched by three million people each broadcast. Can you even imagine that there are that many boring people in the world? But the news was changing quickly, so everybody but me was all abuzz. Rachel sent me a message to order a "hot chart" from the graphics team that displayed the company's losses for the day. The title of the chart was to be "Stock Sinks," and it was needed on air in less than a minute. I made the request, and the graphic was created. Ten seconds later, Hot Andy called for the chart, and it went up.

As it appeared for our audience of three million people, the host of the show, Bill Griffeth, said, "And as you can see by this chart, the stock stinks." And then, he added a panicked, "No, wait—what?"

All of a sudden, there was a five-alarm fire in the control room. Hot Andy shouted, "GO TO COMMERCIAL! GO TO COMMERCIAL!"

"Stock stinks?" Rachel said, incredulously. Turning to me, she fumed: "No! No! Stock siiiinks!! Stock SINKS. Patrick, is that what you ordered?"

I was very confused, because the second the graphic was ordered, I'd gone right back to *E! Online News*. "What?" I asked.

"I told you to order a graphic with the title 'Stock Sinks' and that says, 'Stock STINKS'!"

"Oh," I said. "Shit." And I swear I did everything I could possibly think of to stop what happened next. But suddenly there I was, bent over at the waist laughing so hard that I was actually crying. "Stock stinks. OH, MY GOOOOOODD. STOCK STINKS!!"

As the show came back from the unexpected commercial break and I heard Bill Griffeth begin his formal apology, I was able to compose myself . . . sort of.

"Get out," Rachel said.

"Right," I said, starting to laugh again.

I wasn't sure if I was officially fired or not. But I didn't care. I was done. I grabbed my bag from my desk, jogged to the elevator, checked to make sure the Money Honey was nowhere in sight, got in, and left.

Chapter Five

THREE TERRIBLE DATES . . . AND ONE REALLY GOOD ONE

The day after I walked out of CNBC, I hopped on the PATH train and headed into the city. I had less than $200 in the bank and rent was due in a week. And so I did what all hard-working, desperate-for-cash, young creative types who underestimate the value of health insurance do: I got a restaurant job. I'd headed straight for Greenwich Village because, as our Jersey City landlord's wife had warned, "It's the gay part of town, but don't worry, it's still fun!" Thanks for the tip, lady.

One of the first spots I wandered into was a place called Moomba. I had no idea at the time, but, as one of the first establishments in New York City to be both a restaurant and a nightclub, the place was apparently legendary. "We have to kick Leonardo DiCaprio out *aaaaaall* the time," the hostess told me as I filled out an application. "He's so *baaaaaad*," she giggled. Girlfriend loved a long "a."

I was hired on the spot to be a barback. Bar backing led to bartending, and this set in motion the next ten years of my life. Bartending in New York can be amazing. The money is great, the hours can allow for you to pursue other interests, and sometimes you get to meet people you probably wouldn't meet anywhere else. But you can also get lost in it, and that was my greatest fear—waking up one morning and realizing I'd lost a bunch of years to staying out late, partying, and, like, having too much fun. I had two goals I didn't want to lose sight of: figuring out what I *really* wanted to do with my life and finding myself a husband.

The husband part, somehow, seemed less daunting. So the day I turned twenty-eight, I decided to give myself the best birthday present any single, bored, suddenly desperate-to-be-in-a-relationship homosexual could ask for: a Match.com profile. At the time, Match .com was your best option for finding love if you were hoping to avoid the disheartening bar scene. And bear in mind that this was before the widespread adoption of what we euphemistically call "dating" apps—also known as what they really are: "fucking" apps. Just a few years later, my single friends would be swapping dick pics on Grindr and Scruff, apps that could literally geotarget other horny dudes on the prowl and tell you the actual number of feet away they were. It's DoorDash for dick.

I could pretend to be jealous of this kind of precision-guided hookup technology, but really I was relieved to already be locked down by then. I was not made for that world. The idea of, like, posing my penis, taking a picture of it, and then just like *sending* it *around the INTERNET?* It still doesn't make sense to me. *Where's the romance?*

No, at twenty-eight, I signed up for Ye Olde Match.com to find long-term love, plain and simple. My early to midtwenties had been a messy, though occasionally fun, series of casual hookups, falling in love with friends who were . . . not interested, and chasing straight guys who would occasionally get a little handsy a few drinks in. Now, I'd decided, it was time to get serious. And I made a promise to myself: I'd treat this like a real priority. I'd be proactive—meaning I'd get on Match every day, husband shop, and reach out to at least one person. Also, I decided that I'd go on a date with just about anyone who asked me.

Plus, I had a good feeling about my chances. I was a catch. Or, I should say, I had *become* a catch. In the months leading up to my birthday, I had gotten myself into the best shape of my life. I had become Hot Patrick. I looked *good*. Pre-Hot Patrick had done okay too. On the New York City Gay Men's Hotness Scale, you can actually get yourself pretty far as a strong 6 with a great personality. But just prior to becoming Hot Me, things had stalled. One guy, on what I thought was our third date, put his hand on my shoulder when I went in for what I felt was a long overdue first kiss, and said, "Oh nooooooo!" with a shy laugh. This genuinely startled me. I reared my head back to see what was wrong. "Sweetie, I only date hot guys," he said, looking past me to see if there were any in the vicinity. "You understand, right?" Not only did I nod, but I also Paid. For. The. Dinner.

And yes, fuck that guy, but this was a turning point for me. It's true that gay male beauty standards are stupid and impossible, but still, I became determined in that moment to somehow, someway, get hot. And let me tell you, it was an absolutely miserable journey and I do not recommend it. I was eating fewer than 1,800 calories a day, drinking (despite my unusually overactive bladder—more on that later) eighty ounces of water a day like a fucking *camel,* and running—wait for it—five miles, five times a week. And I know we don't really have time to dive into this now, but like *what the hell is wrong with people who enjoy living like this?* You know who I'm talking about. You probably accidentally have a few of these people in your life: the ones who look forward to going to the gym, the ones who always have a water bottle with them everywhere (!!) they go. Water is for mixing with Scotch. I thought everybody knew that. Like, do I want to be healthy enough to live to see my grandkids? Most days, yes. But if I have to drink a bathtub full of water daily, I say fuck them. Grampy tried. I'll leave you a little something when I go (did I mention that this book makes a great gift?).

Anyway, I got myself down to about 170 pounds, with a waistline in the low thirties and my first-ever flat stomach. These were three things I'd dreamed of my entire life, and I knew for fucking sure that my time with them was limited. So I put on my tightest white T-shirt, a pair of army-green cargo shorts, and a black-and-white beanie hat. Then I put my digital camera on the highest shelf I could find and aimed it down at myself. I sucked in my cheeks to show off my limited-time jawline and then held my hands together behind my back to really stretch that MEDIUM-sized, thank you very much, T-shirt over my lean frame.

And I gotta say, the pictures were hot. These days I get a lot of Sean Astin comparisons. But, like, chunky Sean Astin from *The Lord of the Rings.* So in the Hot Me pictures, imagine a young, hot Sean Astin. We're talking underdog football-playing *RUDY* Sean Astin. *That* is how hot I was. Close your eyes, picture it, and DROOL!

But the pictures were also a lie. Like, gay camel marathoner . . . is not me. I knew that I did not have the ability—or even the *desire* if I'm being honest—to maintain that hot body beyond picture day. *It doesn't matter*, I told myself as I uploaded the pictures to my Match .com profile and immediately ordered Dominos—One-click Express Ordered actually, since I had the meal saved as "the usual." *Ahhh! It was good to be back!* I'd find my man and then fall back on my personality! My charm! The hot body pics were just to get me in the door, and once I was there, Mr. Right would love me for *me*! The trim waist wouldn't be so important, right? Oh lesbian upbringing, with your body positivity—how you lead me astray . . .

And then I wrote up a profile to match this Hot Patrick:

> *Hi! I'm Patrick! I'm 27 years old. I love to exercise and eat clean! I love to read books and go to the theater. I'm close with my family, but not too close hahahahaha. I'm also a mixologist at an upscale steakhouse, so I know my way around a good meal and fancy wine list. If this sounds interesting to you, give me a shout. Let's go on a hike and get to know each other better!*

I instinctively clicked "average" in the body type section, then chuckled at my mistake. In an act of earned bravery, I clicked "athletic build" and then pushed "submit" before I could panic and reconsider.

Oh how I cringe rereading that profile now. *Eat clean! Mixologist? Give. Me. A. Shout. LET'S GO ON A HIKE?* It honestly reads as though

I'd been taken hostage and was sending coded messages through a proof-of-life statement. Like, who *is* that person.

Anyway, bait set, I started to get some nibbles.

Some terrible, terrible nibbles.

The first bad date was my fault. Or at least mostly my fault. Jeremy was twenty-six and worked "in finance," which meant that after we got married, I could probably quit my job and stay home with the dogs or whatever. I was thin now; anything was possible!

For our first date, I drove down to pick him up at his East Village apartment. My assumption, even though we had yet to meet in real life, was that if things went well, I'd be moving in in a few weeks, so I wanted to take a peek at his place before we drove up to Fort Tryon Park at the northern tip of Manhattan to go for a walk. Perfect first-date shit.

And yes, at this point in my life, I owned a car for the first time. A friend of my mom's had given it to me for free, so why not? Not that this meant anything to me then or now, but it was a gray 2002 Buick Century with 210,000 miles on it. What do literally any of those words mean?

Everyone in my life had tried to talk me out of owning a car. There was absolutely no reason for me, a Manhattanite, to have a car: The insurance and upkeep would cost a fortune, and I'd be reliant on street parking—the rules of which are taken very seriously in New York City. Every morning I'd have to get up and move my car before 8 AM or risk a ticket. *I was a bartender, and a little bit of a partier*, my friends and roommates all reminded me. *There was no WAY I was going to wake up every morning and do the responsible thing.*

They were right, of course. And as a result, the parking tickets started stacking up. At $96 a pop. And what seems truly insane about for the Hanson brothers, I was going to be hobnobbing with icons like these whose celebrity would never fade . . .

I told all my college friends that I'd been selected for this coveted internship out of the hundreds of people who applied for it. This was definitely not true. I found out later that I was the only college kid they interviewed who was willing to show up at 5 AM to prep for the 6 AM start time. And as far as being around famous people . . . that also wasn't a thing. Yes, big stars like Madonna and George Clooney were on *Matty in the Morning* all the time—over the phone. Turns out that Hollywood types don't drop by the Bay State as much as you'd think. But by that time, I'd made such a big deal about all the celebrities I'd be meeting that I basically had no choice but to deliver *amazing celebrity stories.*

For example, on my first day as an intern, Jennifer Lopez was on the show to promote the film *Out of Sight* and her upcoming debut album. And even though I was brand new, I was the one selected to meet J.Lo and her team at the radio station's parking lot. "She was much tinier than I expected," I told my friends later, hoping that J.Lo was, in fact, tiny. Because, obviously, she had called in from the West Coast, not actually showed up at the station in Boston. But there was no way any of my friends would be up early enough to hear the interview and know that. "And she was very sweet," I continued. "Before I could even introduce myself, she said, 'You must be Patrick, the new guy. Don't worry. I'll be gentle.'" Can you fucking imagine?!

A few weeks into the internship, Gwyneth Paltrow was on the show (she wasn't). Her interview was in the 9 AM block, but she arrived at 8 AM. I was sent to the lobby to meet her.

"Oh Patrick, I really wanted to get bagels for everyone," she said. "I hate to arrive empty-handed."

it to me, as I sit here writing this now, is that I never even considered paying them. I was making about $200 a night at my bartending job; in what world was I gonna spend half of that the next day on a parking ticket? Especially since I was already deep in default on my student loans at the time—that's a fun little wrinkle!—where was I supposed to get all this money?

And then, of course, came the letter informing me that my driving privileges had been revoked and would remain revoked until the tickets were paid. But did this stop me from driving? NOPE! How was I supposed to get Jeremy to Fort Tryon Park? By subway? I double-parked outside his building and ran up to his apartment to take a look. Nice, but we'd for sure need something bigger once the baby came. We hopped back in the car, and off we went.

Jeremy was *very* cute; he had a swimmer's build that reminded me of Logan from Walnut Hill. He had Logan-style curly blond hair. He was about the same height as Logan. His eyes were a similar blue to Logan's. He, um . . . looked a lot like Logan. But Jeremy was more than just a near-perfect Logan look-alike; he was ambitious, apparently very out at his corporate finance job, which—sexy! And he too had been to Every. Last. Lilith. Fair! Match.com, for date number one, you are knocking it out of the park. This was going great.

But then it happened. Just as I got onto the West Side Highway, a cop pulled up behind me. I froze.

"What's wrong?" Jeremy asked, sensing the change.

"Ahhhh, hopefully nothing," I said, my eyes glued to the rearview mirror. But then the lights and siren started, and I knew the jig was up.

"Fuck," I said. "FUCK FUCK FUCK FUCK FUCK."

"Were you speeding?" Jeremy asked, as I pulled over. Now I could hear a little bit of panic rising in *his* voice.

"NO," I shouted.

"Then why are you being pulled over? Are you, like, wanted or something?"

"No. Well, maybe?" I said.

"WHAT," Jeremy said, finally turning down the Indigo Girls just as they were getting to the chorus of "Closer to Fine." Insult to injury.

I turned off the car. "Look, Jeremy: I like you. But before we take any next steps, there's something you need to know . . . I have like a hundred outstanding parking tickets. I'm not supposed to be driving. My license has been suspended and . . . I think I might be getting arrested." I started sobbing.

You have to understand something about me: I live in complete fear of getting in trouble for anything. I am a total rule follower. This "Fuck the Man, I'm not paying my parking tickets" situation was . . . a departure for me. Who I really am is the kid who would beg other kids to stop talking in class so the teacher wouldn't yell. I'm the friend who refused to sneak into movies I didn't pay for. I'm the nerd who was always home ten minutes before curfew, and I'm still the adult apartment dweller who never once tried to steal his neighbor's Wi-Fi. I wasn't this skinny (ish) bad boy whose devil-may-care atti-tude was about to send him to p r i s o n! I was husband material— responsible and at heart a good person!

Jeremy's demeanor turned icy. He was no longer the nice, Indigo Girl–loving twink he'd been ten minutes ago. "Calm down," he growled. And then, for good measure, he yelled it: "CALM DOWN!" The yelling was unexpected. But somehow, sexy?

"Here's what's going to happen," he said. "They're gonna run your plates. They're gonna see that you're driving with a suspended license, and you're gonna be in big fucking trouble. If you STAY FUCKING

CALM, they might just impound your car, give you a ticket, and let us go."

"Okay," I said, gathering myself. *How did he know all this?*

"But you've gotta stay calm! Because if you freak out, and they search us, we're BOTH going to jail."

"Wait," I said. "Why would YOU go to jail?"

"Because of the bag of fucking COCAINE I have in my pocket," he whisper-screamed.

It felt as though time stopped. I felt woozy. How could I be sitting in a car with a . . . *drug user?* You see, I have an admittedly irrational fear of drugs. Especially cocaine. This is 100 percent tied to the '80s-era Nancy Reagan "Just Say No" campaign. Of course, I *now* know that the "war on drugs" was a racist attack on Black and brown people that destroyed families and entire communities writ large. But I gotta tell you, at the time, THAT SHIT WORKED ON ME. The night before my first day of sixth grade, I ran sobbing into my mother's bedroom because little gay me was *convinced* some mean eighth-grade boys would try to get me to do cocaine with them, and when refused, would DRAG ME INTO THE BATHROOM, HOLD ME DOWN, AND *INJECT* ME WITH IT. Because, as Nancy Reagan taught us, it was all about getting a newbie *hooked.* Once I was hooked, I was theirs. Those eighth grade boys would own me, and I would do whatever I had to do—whatever they'd make me do—to get the juice. And while, of course, nothing like this ever happened, I spent my middle school and high school years on high alert for the dreaded "peer pressure" that was the first step to ruin. That's why I had dressed in drag for my *Go Ask Alice* report; I wanted to warn others off this dangerous path. I, for one, wouldn't be tricked into becoming a teenage alcoholic or drug addict. I would just say "NO." As you can imagine, I was a ton of fun.

"You brought *cocaine* on our first date?" I asked, incredulously. "That's so . . . unromantic! I don't do *DRUGS*. Don't you know you can die or become addicted the *FIRST* time you try them?" I was all up in my Nancy Reagan talking points now. And I was *mad*.

"Keep your voice down!" Jeremy hissed, craning to look at the cops, still sitting in their cruiser behind us, probably calling for backup. "I didn't bring it for *us*. I'm meeting friends later."

"You made plans for after our first date!?" I screamed.

"What? Yes! Why are you yelling?"

"Because I'm taking you to Fort Tryon Park . . . that place is SPE-CIAL. What if we discovered we were soulmates or something?" I was spiraling. But the fact that he hadn't even left room for the possibility that we might become immediately inseparable really hurt my feelings. Which I know is insane. But . . . if he kicked the cocaine habit . . . maybe there was a future for us? In one last desperate attempt to rekindle our connection, I reached for his hand and said, "Jeremy, I'm scared."

The only word that accurately describes what he did next is "recoil." He moved as far away from me as possible and said, "I think this date was a bad idea."

One of the officers came up to the car. After running my license and registration, he asked both Jeremy and me to step out. I assumed I was smelling my last whiffs of free air for a while.

"I'm sure you know we have to take the car," the cop said. "And these are for you." He handed me a stack of freshly written tickets. I immediately put them in my bag, never to be seen again. We stood there for a minute.

"Wait, are we free to go?" I asked.

"Yup," the cop said. "And to get your car back, you need to—"

"Nah, you can keep it," I said, assuming that would be the end of it. I . . . had not yet learned my lesson. And I never did get the car back. Though I did, eventually, have to pay over $5,000 in fines and legal fees in order to restore my license. Which I only did because I needed an ID to get into bars. Because, priorities.

With the cops gone, things were looking up. Maybe we could salvage this thing! I turned to Jeremy and said, "Hey! So we could still try to—"

"NO," he said. "Absolutely not. Whatever it is you're about to ask me, the answer is no. Whichever way you're walking, I'm going the other way."

And because I couldn't think of anything else to say, I just shouted, "You shouldn't do drugs! They're . . . BAD for you!" And I turned and left.

. . . .

Things didn't get better after that. I had paid for a full year of Match .com and the clock was ticking. If I didn't find a husband by the time they tried (and failed) to charge my card again, that was it for me. Future Me would probably die old and alone.

Around this time, there was an awkwardly cute actor who was making a name for himself on Broadway. He was in a show that I had seen and loved, and for some reason, I hadn't been able to take my eyes off of him. It's hard to describe this guy's magnetism on stage. I mean, Logan Hughes he is not. So it wasn't so much about his looks as it was his vulnerability and sweet shyness. He had a quiet star power that just sort of drew the eye to him.

Anyway, it turned out that this actor was a friend of a friend, so our mutual friend showed him my Match.com pictures and the actor agreed to be set up on a blind date. The plan was for the two of us to meet up for happy hour at a Lower East Side gay bar that we both liked. I was trying not to get ahead of myself, but I was excited. Just from what I'd seen on stage, I imagined him to be quirky and a little weird, but in an adorable kind of way. He'd be on the quiet side, so it'd take a little work to get him talking, but I was up for the challenge.

As I walked up to the place, I saw him standing outside and headed straight toward him. His reaction to seeing me was not what I expected. Have you ever been in a situation where you meet some- one for the first time—or more like when someone meets *you* for the first time—and you can tell that they are instantly disappointed? Like, I understand if you hate me after we've gotten to know one another, but this guy soured immediately. My steamy, strategically angled Match.com pics had only been taken a few months prior, but in that time I had certainly reacquainted myself with the joy of eating. So as I walked up, he did a quick up-and-down body scan (EVERYONE SEES YOU WHEN YOU DO THIS—IT CANNOT BE DONE SUBTLY) and then he actually *frowned*—WHICH IS SOMETHING YOU CANNOT DO BY ACCIDENT. IT ACTUALLY TAKES EFFORT AND MUSCLE MOVEMENT TO DO THAT WITH YOUR MOUTH.

"Hi, I'm Patrick," I said, cheerily sticking out a hand.

"hello," he said, lowercase *h* intended. He did not introduce him- self or, like, receive my hand for shaking. For just a second, I actually thought he was just going to turn and walk away. Which, I gotta say, would have made for a hilarious moment here. Instead, he turned and walked into the bar. I honestly wasn't sure if he wanted me to follow or not. Or, more like, it was clear that he did *not* want me to follow, but if I didn't, I was the rude one, right? *No way*, I thought, *it's not going down like that.*

Once inside, we sat at the bar. We each ordered a drink, and I started a one-sided conversation that quickly just turned into an interview about his career and accomplishments. Where I had been expecting sweet shyness, I was getting disappointed boredom. Where was the magnetism he displayed onstage? He couldn't even *pretend* he was interested in having a conversation with me? After about thirty minutes of questioning, I excused myself to go to the bathroom to regroup. What a dud! But they can't all be winners, right? Our mutual friend had spoken so highly of him; maybe we had gotten off to a bad start. I splashed some water on my face and headed back out there.

But he was gone. Apparently, in the time it took me to pee and wash my hands, he had made his exit.

I'd love to say that that was the last I ever heard of that guy. That, talented as he was, he vanished into oblivion never to work again. Unfortunately, that's not true. In fact, this guy would go on to star in one of the longest-running and most beloved TV sitcoms of all time. Yes, it was Jerry Seinfeld. I kid. But this is why I haven't given you any sort of physical description of him here—it would be a dead giveaway. Honestly, I'd *love* to just tell you who he is—it would make this story that much funnier. But we have mutual friends, and I really don't want to deal with bitchy secondhand texts where he denies this. Because it *happened*. And he was a dirtbag! And he was Matt LeBlanc. Just kidding, just kidding. But note to anyone planning on becoming famous: Be nice to everyone. You never know who will end up with a successful podcast that results in a book deal where they tell the story about the time you were mean to them. And who will probably name your name at an upcoming live show.

• •

Things seemed a little more promising the night I met Ricky at one of my favorite Village bars downtown, a place called Pieces. Pieces is a mess, but a wonderful mess. It's the kind of place where the music is always too loud, the floor is always too sticky, and the drinks are always too strong. In short, IT'S FABULOUS. Perfect for a no-longer skinny-hot guy like me to drink alone. There's no expectation that you "look nice" or "aren't drunk." You just come to get wasted, scream/listen to the gay hits on the jukebox, and maybe hook up with an unmemorable stranger you'll never see again.

Which is why Ricky stood out. He was very hot—tall and slender with olive skin and curly brown hair. He had a big, beautiful smile and sparkly brown eyes. I'd never seen him at Pieces before, but he was sort of working the room—maybe he was a new manager or something? I watched him move from table to table saying hi to everyone, hoping he'd eventually come to me at the bar. He did.

"Hi," he said, sitting down next to me. "I'm Ricky!"

"Hi," I replied. "I'm Patrick." The music was loud, so he leaned into me as we began a very easy conversation.

Do I need to point out what we all know by now? I like a cocktail. And I can generally hold my liquor. But as the night went on and we continued to drink—all on my tab—things got . . . hazy. One minute we were talking, the next minute we were making out at the bar and then the next thing I knew, we were in a cab heading to my place. My self-esteem is fine, I promise; so I'm not ashamed to admit how excited I was that this guy who was WAY out of my league seemed to truly be into me.

Anyway, I don't have a complete picture of what happened when we got back to my apartment. But rest assured, we had a lot of very hot, very consensual, very gay sex. And we'll just leave it at that; we'll have to, because unfortunately I was so wasted, I don't remember the incredibly sordid details. When it was over, Ricky seemed like he was getting ready to leave, but I asked him if he wanted to stay the night.

"Hmm, I don't usually do that, but it is late. I guess if you don't mind?"

"I definitely do not mind," I said, as he climbed back into bed and we both passed out.

When I woke up the next morning, Ricky was still there. He was still naked, and he still smelled amazing. *Was he my boyfriend now???* I nuzzled my head into his shoulder and started thinking about clearing out some closet space for him. A minute later, he opened his eyes and looked at me. He was for sure more confused than I wanted him to be.

"Good morning, handsome," I said.

"Hi," he said kindly, as he moved away from me, rose from bed, and got dressed. And then he said the words I'll never forget as long as I live: "So, just a reminder, are you still good to go to the ATM? It's two hundred dollars."

I stared at him wide-eyed and silent for like ten seconds as little bits and pieces of the night before came back to me. "Yuuuuuuuuu-uuuuuuuup," I said slowly, wanting to be agreeable. I guess I did remember him saying something about money in the . . . throes of our . . . lovemaking, but my attention had been focused elsewhere . . . and OH MY GOD, WAIT, RICKY IS TOTALLY A SEX WORKER.

We walked to the corner bodega in awkward silence. I punched in my code and checked my balance: $212. I tapped "Withdrawal" and handed my life savings over to Ricky.

"Don't worry," he said as he folded the bills and put the money in his pocket. "I promise it was worth it."

. . . .

A few weeks before my Match.com subscription expired, my friend Ellyn pulled up my profile. Clicking through the pictures, she said, "Oh my God, remember when you were skinny for a week?" And then, "This is the worst profile I've ever read."

She took it upon herself to rewrite the entire thing. Maybe she thought that she had a better handle than I did on what made me attractive. Or maybe she just feared that if I ended up an old crank, she'd be the one bringing me my TV dinners in my sad studio apartment full of cats.

I paid no attention. My subscription was almost up. I'd gone on a bunch of terrible dates and I was DONE. I'd be alone forever, my looks—which I'd had for all of two weeks—had already faded, and my personality . . . well, ha! Let's just say that nobody was that interested in an overconfident, perpetually broke hot mess. If Ellyn wanted to waste her time on a lost cause, that was her problem. It wouldn't matter what she wrote—I was destined to be alone. What's the male version of a "spinster"? A "himster"?

A few weeks later, I got an email on my Yahoo! account. (I . . . might not be young.) Apparently, someone on Match.com named "Steve" had messaged me. I clicked on the picture and—look at that—he was cute! I tried to open the message, but I couldn't unless I signed up for another year of Match.com. Not a chance in hell.

Several weeks passed. One day, while I was checking my email at a local internet café—children, I've only been allotted 60,000 words for this book, so I do not have the space to explain; just know that the early 2000s were *wild*—anyway, when I went to my MySpace page (sigh), I saw that I had a message: "Hello from Steve from Match." It read:

> Hey Patrick! I reached out to you a few weeks ago on Match .com but didn't hear anything back. Since your friend Ellyn included your full name in the profile she wrote, I figured I'd do a search on MySpace and see if I could find you here! Anyway, you're cute and you sound NORMAL, so give me a shout if you want to meet for a drink!

Of course, I'd never read the profile Ellyn had rewritten ("normal"?), and so I had no idea that she'd broken the number one rule of online dating: Do not use a full name. I'd be mad at her later, I decided. This guy was cute and clearly obsessed with me. Also, I was out of cash and watching the timer tick down on my (internet café) computer. I needed to respond quickly.

"Look at you, Inspector Gadget!" I wrote back, trying to sound *fun* and *cool* and not at all like this was the first time ever that someone else was pursuing me. "I'd love to meet up some time," I wrote, trying to sound nonchalant. "I'm headed out of town for a week tomorrow"—which was true—"maybe next week when I'm back?" Writing *"How about TONIGHT? Or right now even? And then we can text every five minutes while I'm on vacation???"* seemed like a bit much. So no big deal, the week after!

Steve insists that the week came and went and that I didn't follow up with him. This seems . . . very unlike me. But in any event, one of us reached back out to the other, and, on August 24, 2007, Steve and I had our first date—a lunch date, because we aren't sluts.

The plan was to meet at a restaurant in Hell's Kitchen called Vynl at 1 PM. Since I was due at my bartending job at four, it seemed like just enough time to suss out whether we hated each other or whether we'd eventually marry. Vynl had a big floor-to-ceiling window in front, so my plan was to casually walk past it, try to catch a glimpse of Steve, and then decide whether to stay or run away screaming. You have to understand: I was extremely nervous because Steve, at least in his photos, was *very* good-looking. And *his* photos were *recent*. All he knew of me were my year-old, thin-for-a-week pics. No, I hadn't totally let myself go, but I was also not in the mood for another disappointed grimace upon meeting. And if all of this sounds very superficial to you, then you are reading this correctly; single gay men are terrifying.

I walked past the window, trying to look casual and not at all like I was there to appraise the guy waiting for me at the bar. "Please be ugly, please be ugly, please be ugly," I muttered to myself. The pressure of a meal with a hot person—the sheer exhaustion of trying to be charming enough for both of us—was just not something I was in the mood for. But then, boom: eye contact. The guy sitting at the bar looked up from what I would later learn was the *New York Times* crossword puzzle (swoon) at that exact moment and busted me staring at him. And sorry, Hinds, no dice; I couldn't not try to make this one work. This guy was fucking hot. Early on in our relationship, for some insane reason, I used to try to describe Steve's own face to him and why I found it so sexy. Here's all I could ever come up with: He has very defined features—deep-set eyes, a strong chin, and pale, smooth skin. His face is expressive even when he doesn't mean it to be.

Anyway, I'd been caught. He stood up and waved. I had to go in.

"Hi," he said. His voice was deep and welcoming. He was actually excited to meet me.

"Hi, nice to meet you!" I replied. We hugged, lingering juuuuuust enough to show mutual interest. So far, so good.

Once we were seated, we pretended to look over the menus, but we both knew we'd be ordering salads. Because gay first date. And we ordered iced teas—unsweetened, obviously.

The salads were dropped and we pretended they were *amazing*. The conversation was going well—small talk developed into interesting medium talk—but I wanted more, some kind of conversation that would take this thing to the next level. So I was brave.

"All right, handsome," I said. "Tell me something you've never told anyone on a first date."

"Hmm," he said, amused at my boldness. "Should I tell you about my ex-wife?"

"WHAT???" I yodeled. This was perfect. This was it (!). I mean, I had a million questions now, but somehow this was the Perfect Piece of Information to share to tell me he was *in*. I thought I had been bold, but he was upping the ante by telling me some major life information here. This was not the kind of bomb you drop on a guy you never plan to see again, right?

The server popped in at this exact moment. "How are we doing?" she asked. Steve and I both burst out laughing.

"We're having a *great* first date," I said, eyeing Steve to gauge his reaction.

"It's true," he said. "But I think we need some cocktails?"

"OH MY GOD, MARRY ME NOW," I shouted, as we placed our drink orders.

"Well, about that ex-wife . . . we were young, we met in college," Steve continued. "I wasn't out or even sure who I was. But she's beautiful and wonderful and we're still friends."

"Wow."

"Okay, your turn."

"Should I tell you about the time I almost got arrested for a bunch of unpaid parking tickets?" I asked.

After lunch, Steve asked if he could walk me to work, and when I said yes, he slipped his hand into mine and led the way. To this day, that remains one of the sexiest and boldest things I've ever experienced. And I gotta say, fifteen years later, I still think of us like that. Hand in hand. Partners. He's always there to pull me in the right direction or at least make sure I don't stray too far off track. I'm so lucky that I don't have to go on any more terrible dates. Steve, I love you so much. Please bear that in mind when you get home tonight and find a sink full of my breakfast dishes. And the coffee creamer still on the counter.

. . . .

I should end the chapter there, but I told you I am extra. Plus, if I ended it there, I would be leaving out the most legendary part of this day. Steve came back to see me at the bar toward the end of my shift and invited me to go with him to a late-night musical theater open mic at the Laurie Beechman Theatre—a space in the basement of a Theater District restaurant. Booze! Show tunes! My new hot number! I was in.

At this open mic, aspiring performers brought their own sheet music and then performed their song live on stage, accompanied by a pianist. We were two or three drinks in when one of the final names of the evening was called, and suddenly a gorgeous six-foot-five-inch-tall Black man appeared onstage, wearing 1980s-style workout short shorts and a very tight white tank top. He had no sheet music; instead, he carried a large boom box. "I'll be singing 'Big Black Man' from *The Full Monty*," he told the emcee. *The Full Monty* is, of course, the musical based on the hit indie film about a group of ordinary men who create a male striptease act to make money after losing their jobs. And of course, the song "Big Black Man" is an homage to one character's large penis.

It was a little after midnight and everyone in the room—the performer in short shorts included—were more than a few drinks in. The epically sober emcee nervously assessed the situation. "Okay," he said. "But we don't want you getting us shut down, so please—let's keep most of our clothes on . . ."

The performer was not paying attention. He hit "play" on the boom box's cassette player and started singing the song. He sounded great. He looked even better. As he tore his tank top off, he ripped into the song, delivering a set of lyrics that are exactly as suggestive as you're imagining.

The audience went wild and there was no slowing this guy down. He had the room at a boil, gyrating and dancing as he hit the chorus—a chorus that calls for the man to do something called "the Popcorn."

Now I don't know what "the Popcorn" is, but it seemed to involve pulling one's shorts completely off to reveal an enormous flaccid penis, which he then flounced in such a way that some queen at the next table shrieked, "Oh my god, that's not the Popcorn! BITCH, HE'S DOING THE HELICOPTER!"

As the room devolved into pandemonium around us—the emcee shouting for someone to cut the lights, people jeering and throwing dollar bills at the stage, the performer himself delighting in all of it—Steve leaned over to me and mouthed the words, "I always take you to the nicest places."

Chapter Six

OH, THE PLACES YOU'LL GO

Early on in our relationship, Steve and I were delighted to discover that neither one of us wanted kids. This would eventually change in a moment that is as dramatic and over the top as you've likely come to expect from me, and we'll get there, but for those first few years, we would joke that we'd just name our vacations, instead. We were the proud parents of precocious little Desmond (our trip to Miami) and quiet, shy Belinda (our long weekend in Cancún). And maybe Katherine (our trip to Key West) didn't quite live up to our expectations, but it was still cheaper than private pre-school. Instead of becoming parents, we were determined to become #TravelGays, living a carefree, globe-trotting lifestyle. Even better? Thanks to the generosity of a wealthy friend, we weren't just *regular* #TravelGays—we'd become #FirstClassTravelGays who had gotten used to *very* fancy vacations. This wealthy friend 100 percent does not want me writing about him in this book. Not for any interesting reason, I promise you. He's not a celebrity, or, like a cartel boss; he's just a sweet, rich, slightly older guy who lives a private life. He loves to travel and loves to bring his friends along with him—on his dime. Also, since I referred to him as "slightly older," he's asked me to point out that he's in significantly better shape than me. Which is true. Anyway, he's agreed to let me tell this story as long as I give him a pseudonym. So for our purposes here, we'll call him Dr. Jonathan Newman—a character in his favorite episode of *The Golden Girls* . . . which I know most of you queens already knew.

Dr. Jonathan Newman and I first met at The Duplex, a stalwart gay bar right next door to the legendary Stonewall Inn in Greenwich Village. He was cute and interesting and I thought we should date. He . . . did not agree with that, but was up for a new friend, and so new friends we became.

Dr. J was the first truly rich person I ever knew. He lives in a hip New York neighborhood on the top floor of a restored old factory building. The building elevator opens directly into his apartment. If you don't live in New York City, please reread that sentence and try to fully digest it. It means *his apartment is the entire floor of the building.*

The walls of the apartment are lined with expensive art; we're talking Picassos and Dalís, people. And the living room is big enough for a grand fucking piano; it's truly huge. But the crown jewel of the place is the private roof terrace, which he converted into a Parisian tea garden, complete with an authentic Metro arch and a nineteenth-century working (!) streetlamp, both of which he had imported from France. So yeah, this guy is very rich and unbelievably homosexual. My kinda guy.

Dr. Jonathan Newman and I became very close over the years. I think he enjoyed finally having a friend as sophisticated as he is. LOL.

Just kidding. I must be good company because I'm a living train wreck who has broken upwards of $4,000 worth of glassware and teapots at his home. That is a real number. And I once cracked his marble kitchen countertop while smashing bags of ice against it to make cocktails. But I'm FUN, so Dr. J replaced the counter instead of me.

One afternoon, we were sitting in his garden eating afternoon tea sandwiches and scones with clotted cream—*all of which he made himself*—when he popped the question. Well, *a* question:

"Patch," he said, calling me the only nickname I could ever tolerate. "What are the chances of you coming to meet me in Provence in a few weeks? I'll pay for everything."

"The chances are good, Dr. Jonathan Newman." This was before I had met Steve, and at the time, I was a broke, twenty-five-year-old bartender whose most recent adventure included getting wasted before noon with my friend Mike on the beach in Fire Island. The result of being so wasted was that we forgot to put on sunscreen at any point in the day and got debilitating sun poisoning in that little island town without a doctor. So instead of partying with the gays all night, we went to bed at 6 PM and *prayed out loud to God* that we be allowed to live until morning. After that, my skin peeled off, like a boa constrictor, for two solid weeks. So yeah, Dr. J, I was ready for a classy-ass getaway to the South of France.

The only fly in the ointment was that we'd be sharing a house with a couple of Dr. J's French friends, a mother/adult daughter duo I'm calling Fantine and Cosette, after the French mother/daughter characters in *Les Misérables*. I know most of you got that; I'm just trying to keep Derek in the loop. Hey, handsome. Anyway, Fantine and Cosette were new friends that Dr. J had recently met in New York. Individually, Dr. J said, they were delightful. Fantine, who was around Dr. J's age,

part Aspen ski chalet, one part luxury log cabin. It was huge; I couldn't even see the whole thing from the driveway. I guess that when Dr. J had said "farmhouse" to me, he was using the word "farmhouse" the way other rich people use the word "cottage" to describe their eight-bedroom/six-bathroom beachfront mansion in the Hamptons. Or the way they use the word "babysitter" to describe the caregiver who actually raises their children. Oh, rich people and your humble brags.

"Patrick! We're over here by the pool!" I heard Fantine and Cosette shout.

Turning, I was greeted by four of the largest, palest, roundest breasts I have ever seen. Fantine and Cosette, wearing only bikini bottoms, were jumping and waving at me to join them. Now to be clear, I am not one of those gays who is in any way disgusted by the naked female body—far from it—so what I'm about to say, I say *purely* as an anatomical observation. These. Breasts. Were. Pendulous. Hypnotic. They were at once *clearly* subject to the laws of gravity and yet mightily defying those same laws with their motion, bobbing and weaving and, dare I say, jiggling.

And can I just take a second here to commend the French? The sheer body confidence on display in that moment was pretty inspiring. Neither of these women had flat stomachs or perky boobs, yet here they were, tits out and waving with enthusiasm like teenage cheerleaders in a *Porky's* movie. And as someone who went swimming in a T-shirt well into my twenties, I gotta say, I was impressed, if still a little confused about where I was supposed to look.

The ladies settled back into their pool chairs, breaking the spell. Excusing myself, I took my bags inside and found Dr. J stewing freshly picked black cherries in the kitchen. And let this be a reminder to all of us: international travel is no excuse to not be as gay as you possibly can be wherever you are.

"This morning," Dr. J said, barely looking up as he stirred the pot, "a four-foot snake slithered underneath me while I was reading in the hammock. I didn't even scream. I actually considered dipping my toe into its face and letting it just kill me on the spot." It seemed that the week leading up to my arrival had not gone well.

"Wow," I said. "And I just saw my first four in-person breasts."

"I'm not even sure they brought shirts," Dr. J replied.

That night, the four of us ate dinner outside under an enormous green hackberry tree. On the menu: cheeses, roast chicken, and haricots verts. We sampled all kinds of wine local to the region. I was having, truly, one of the greatest nights of my life. It was 9:30 PM, the sun was still out, and I was wine drunk on a "farm" in the *South of France* instead of mixing martinis for ungrateful finance bros at my steakhouse bartending job. And, blessedly, everybody's breasts remained safely tucked inside their shirts. These women . . . were they my *new best friends?*

It was not to be. When Dr. J returned to the table with vanilla ice cream and the pot of stewed cherries, Fantine's eyes popped wide open and her face darkened. She crossed her arms and sulked.

"Welcome to France, Patch," Dr. J said, setting down a small bottle of chocolate milk in front of me. He knew that chocolate milk was my favorite.

With that, Fantine let out a literal "harrumph" and stormed into the house. I had no idea what was happening, but Cosette seemed to, and didn't want to stick around for it.

"I'm going for a swim," she said, as she unbuttoned her shirt and let her breasts tumble out.

"Oh my Lord," the usually reserved Dr. J muttered.

And then from inside the house, Fantine shouted, "Jonathan, can I speak to you for a minute."

"Don't unpack, Patch," Dr. J said to me, rising from the table. "We're getting out of here first thing in the morning." He strode off into the house. I filled my glass with that wonderful chocolate milk and ladled some cherries onto my ice cream. *This is one of the best nights of my life*, I thought.

A car came for us early the next morning before Fantine and Cosette were up. Apparently, Fantine had started acting weirdly possessive as soon as she found out I was coming to France. That night she'd laid into Dr. J. She was incensed at the fact that they'd been together at the house for a WEEK and he hadn't ONCE made STEWED CHERRIES for HER! And didn't he know that SHE TOO loved chocolate milk? Only an INSENSITIVE PRICK would get chocolate milk for ONE person and not for EVERYONE!

Dr. J left them a note: *Patch and I are off to Paris for a few days. I'll be back by the end of the week.* As the driver loaded our bags into the car, Dr. J laughed hysterically. "I'm not coming back, Patch," he snorted. "I'm free!" And to this day, he has never spoken to either of those women again.

. . . .

That trip was the first of many. Over the years, Dr. Jonathan Newman took me all across the world: London, Paris, Stockholm, Denmark, Istanbul, Budapest—many of these cities, multiple times. And you'd think that these trips would have stopped when Steve came into the picture, but that wasn't the case at all—Steve just got added to the itineraries.

And just because I know you're thinking it, let me address the giant three-way in the room. No, these trips were not paid for by me and/or Steve in weird, kinky, sex stuff. Dr. J never once asked us to smuggle heroin in our rectums or to snatch a kid off the street to funnel into a pedophile ring, although once you get a taste of those first-class British Airways "lay-flat" beds, you'll do almost anything.

So I admit it, we'd turned into first-class travel addicts. The Doc had us hooked on the good stuff, and there was no going back. You see, before Dr. J, I traveled coach like most everyone else. I was the person praying for the petite, ninety-eight-pound lady seatmate, while simultaneously knowing that due to my, um, not petiteness, I'm everyone's nightmare seatmate. One time, I got to my row for a six-hour flight from New York to LA, and the guy in the window seat actually said out loud, "Oh God, not you."

So I get it. Coach is the worst. There's no way to fly coach in comfort; it's always two hundred degrees, the flight attendants treat us like the animals we are, and you've got guys like me hogging the armrests and breathing at you.

That's the hellscape we thought we'd left forever once we started traveling with Dr. Jonathan Newman. Because, you see, he only flies first class. And I gotta tell you, traveling first class is a real eye-opener. Have you ever noticed how you don't see very famous people in airports? Clearly they travel a lot, but you never see them! Like, you're never in the security line behind Lady Gaga. Madonna is never emptying her pockets into a plastic tray in front of you or getting a rough pat down by the same hostile TSA agents. *I don't care that you're the Material Girl, you can't bring more than 3.4 ounces of liquid material in your carry-on!*

This is because these people travel first class. And people traveling in the absolute fanciest first class have *their own entrances at international airports.* Your car drops you off at this entrance, and you walk into a private security area *where you are the only people*. This area is perfectly dimly lit, because this is *First* Class and, what, is Beyonce's skin supposed to tolerate coach-style fluorescent lighting like the rest of us—I mean, *you*? I DON'T THINK SO! Here in First Class, an attendant grabs your checked bags—to be dealt with by someone, *anyone,* but you, and, with the filthy work of baggage handling done, you are whisked away to the private first-class lounge. Please, *help yourself* to the fully stocked bar. Or perhaps you would enjoy a full three-course meal with caviar and wine pairings at any hour of the day. Five thirty AM? Please, have some complimentary 2005 Bodegas Roda Cirsion with your pancakes. And of course, there are celebrities everywhere. Once, Dr. J and I sat next to Charlize Theron and Cate Blanchett sharing a meal in the lounge. Cate, I shit you not, was wearing a nightgown under a fancy silk robe, and a pair of slippers. These were not the pajamas the riffraff in the rest of the airport trudge around in, this was sleepwear of the angels. I mean, you expect Cate Blanchett to wear jeans?

When it's time to board, you are ushered to the gate through a private back hallway. By this time, the poor people have been loaded into steerage, or whatever that area on the other side of The Curtain is called. Don't worry; you will never have to see them. You are shown to your seat, which has the square footage of a medium-sized New York City studio apartment. Did you have a carry-on? No problem. A flight attendant will open your personal closet and deposit it there for you. You will then be offered a pair of pajamas. *Is this a trick? Is it totally gauche to wear the airline-issued PJs?* A quick glance to your left eases your worried mind: Tom Hanks is already wearing his.

For the most part, our trips with Dr. Jonathan Newman had taken us to London, where he had discovered an exclusive boutique hotel in Covent Garden. Even as a bona fide gay-with-no-taste™, I could tell that this hotel was special the first time I laid eyes on it. It's fancy but quaint at the same time. The staff is attentive but not overly doting. It's the kind of place where famous people mix with normies and aren't recognized or bothered.

That's great for them, I guess, but can I just say that I will NEVER understand why celebrities want to be "left alone." What else are you doing it for, if not the attention? As someone who, if I wear my own merch and speak loud enough for my effeminate squawk to be carried on the wind, will *sometimes* be recognized as "that loud gay guy on the podcast my girlfriend makes me listen to," let me just tell you: these moments are sometimes the only reason I get out of bed in the morning. I am Tinker Bell: clap for me, or I will die.

Even though Dr. J doesn't watch movies and hates celebrity culture, he LOVED to book us into this hotel during BAFTA week. The BAFTAs are the British equivalent of the Oscars, and the place was so packed with celebrities that the sheer concentration of celebrity energy in that place turned even Dr. J into a celebrity gawker. There's just something fascinating and memorable about watching famous people do normal things. Why should I still remember the exact outfit Heath Ledger was wearing the day he picked up his dry-cleaning when I was working as a hotel concierge in 2005? No good reason, but I do: It was the full *Brokeback Mountain*, cowboy hat and all. Just kidding. It was a mustard-yellow sweater, distressed blue jeans, sunglasses, and a pair of Chuck Taylors. That mustard-yellow sweater . . . hugged his body. ANYWAY.

One morning, Steve and I were having breakfast in the London hotel restaurant when Kevin Bacon walked in and sat at the table right next to us, facing me. I gotta tell you, Kevin Bacon, who was easily in his mid- to late-fifties at the time, was still eminently sexy. Remember Tommy Lee's body in his infamous sex tape with Pamela Anderson? Lean and tight like a lesbian CrossFit instructor? Kevin Bacon had a body like that, hiding under his clothes of course. And with the hair of an eighteen-year-old internet gay-for-pay California surfer bro, he was really doing it for me that morning. And he drank his coffee black. Hot. Mmm, Kevin!

Just then, someone rudely interrupted my ogling: Frances McDormand. Um, okay Frances McDormand! She just walked right in and sat down to eat breakfast with Kevin Bacon. I don't need to describe to you what Frances McDormand looks like, do I? I mean, this is the woman who wore a jean jacket to the Tony Awards. The year she fucking *won*. She transcends clothes and looks and, okay, she was wearing a sweater dress and jeans and brown suede boots, and how did she make that work so well? But the point is, she is 100 percent *attitude*. She also has four Academy Awards, three BAFTAs, three Golden Globes, two Emmys, and a Tony, and here she was sipping coffee, right next to me, with 2001's Blockbuster Entertainment Award–winning Favorite Actor-Science Fiction Kevin Bacon. What's your game, Bacon? How are you and my Fran having breakfast together? And oh my God, what if I could sneak a picture of Kevin Bacon eating bacon? My gay brain was melting down.

That night, Dr. J, Steve, and I were posted up at the bar to celebrity spot. Kevin and Francis wandered in. *We geeeeeeeeeet it*, you two are *boooooost frooooooonds!* But, new famous people, please! And just when it seemed like it was going to be a slow night, suddenly Dame. Judi. Dench. Walked. In.

We three queens at the bar did an audible gay-gasp: the uniquely homosexual, involuntary response to finding oneself, suddenly, in the presence of an Icon. "Get out of the way, Bacon!" Dr. J muttered through gritted teeth, straining to see past the *Flatliners* star.

Dame Judi Dench was draped in a gorgeous black evening gown but was otherwise hard to get a good look at because she was surrounded by handlers. She and her group were seated at a table and, unfortunately, she was positioned with her back to us. I knew I had to make a move. I mean, this was why we were here, right? To celebrity gawk! I wasn't going to do anything crazy, like approach the table, gush that I was a fan, and strong-arm her into a selfie—I'm a New Yorker, damn it! We know how to handle ourselves around celebrities. I just wanted one good gawk: a straight-on, full-face unobstructed gawk to capture the moment. So I hopped off my stool and headed for the door that led down to the bathrooms. I took the long way around, ignoring Bacon and McDormand like the common street trash they'd suddenly become. Giving Dench's table a wide berth, I noted the *very interesting* coat of arms on the wall and took a moment gazing at it. Uttering a performative "Huh!" I turned around just at her twelve o'clock, allowing myself a sustained look directly into her face. I gay-gasped again: *the eyebrows were meticulous!* Boom. Mission accomplished.

I actually did have to pee, so I opened the door and walked down the narrow flight of stairs leading to the bathrooms. I finished and headed back up the stairs, and when I was about two steps from the top, the door opened. There was Dench, in all her regal elegance, looking somewhat surprised to see the stairs ahead, and more than a little bit uncertain about her ability to navigate them. I, of course, was frozen. My instinct was to back down the stairs to make room for her, but then it also felt sort of rude to just abandon her there. Why hadn't any of the fourteen fucking people at her table thought to accompany this living international treasure to the restroom?

"Young man," she said to me.

"Ma'am?" I squeaked, conjuring the only British-sounding word I could think of.

"Would you be so kind?" she asked, as she folded her arm in such a way that implied I should take it and help guide her down the stairs.

Standing there at the top of the staircase, I felt immediately light-headed. What if Dame Judi Dench took my arm and I passed out, yanking her forward and sending her tumbling to her death? I could see tomorrow's headline:

SWEATY GAY IDIOT MURDERS BAFTA-NOMINATED ICON IN LOO STAIRWELL

I slipped my arm through hers and, because of the awkward position, carefully began to walk backwards down the steps as she walked forward. This wasn't the most elegant procession, but we made our slow, unsteady descent. Now I was getting a bit more of that full-face gawk than I had bargained for, alternating between eye contact with her face and her regal bosom as I backtracked the twenty-two steps down to the loo. And, I guess I could have tried to make conversation ("You're going to love the bathrooms in this place"), and yes, I know she's not the actual queen, but she's played one enough times that it felt wrong to initiate conversation unless I was first spoken to. Which I was not.

When we finally reached the bottom, I bowed my head and mustered the courage to say, "It's been an honor."

"Mmm-hmm," Dame Judi Dench muttered. And then she wandered off, very likely to take a poop. I didn't wait around to escort her back up, and that's the last I saw of her. Perhaps she's still down there.

Chapter Seven

AND THEN THERE WERE THREE

Have you ever walked face-first into a closed glass door, thought for a moment that you had died, and upon realizing you're still alive, reevaluated all your major life choices? Have you ever thought "I want a baby" as glass suddenly shattered around your face?

No?

Well, it happened to me, during a terrible trip to Barcelona; let's call it "Charlie." Barcelona is a true Mediterranean paradise, but by the time Steve and I got there, we were unimpressed. You see, after so many years of Dr. J–funded, all-expenses-paid, first-class travel, Steve and I decided it was time for us to take a trip on our own—and on our own dime. And in the immortal words of Julia Roberts from *Pretty Woman,* this was a big mistake. Huge.

Our first stop was Paris, where we'd booked a little hotel in the Latin Quarter. The Ritz it was not, but our room was small and cute, with a set of French doors that opened to a Juliet balcony overlooking the neighborhood's main boulevard. Paris: you're charming.

The real trouble started on day two. We'd decided to take a day trip out to a little town called Giverny, about ninety minutes outside Paris, to see the home and gardens of Claude Monet. We booked a tour with a local company and loaded into a bus with all the other overweight, visor- and fanny-pack-wearing Americans. As this company dropped off a busload of us at the estate gate at nine in the morning, they told us they'd be back to collect us at five fucking PM. Apparently, the word "tour" in French means "to abandon in a foreign land." Reader, when I tell you that you can see every single thing there is to see there in less than an hour, I'm not exaggerating. I mean, as soon as they let us in, our entire group made a mad waddle to the little pond that was Monet's inspiration for his Water Lilies paintings. It took us all of fourteen minutes to walk around that thing. And then . . . that was it. That was all there was to see. It was 9:14 AM, the bus wasn't coming back until five, and we were out of things to do. We took another look at the water lilies. *Yeah, I guess they really do look different when the light changes.* And *Oh, yeah, that's the little bridge.* But then we were done.

I know some of you have done this tour better somehow and are horrified at what you are reading. But, um, I've seen ponds before. I get it. And I actually think it's a little *weird* that he kept painting the same thing over and over. You don't ever want to paint a *dog* or something? You're in France; paint a baguette or a mime for fuck's sake. And also, if Steve Tipton says there was nothing else to do there, trust that there was nothing else to do there. He spent most of the previous day looking for a coupon for the attraction, and there's absolutely no way he would have let a single euro of our entrance fee go to waste. Sorry, Monet's garden, you are a bust.

We finally got back to Paris around 7 PM and hopped on the Metro to head back to our hotel. It was hot and I was looking forward to a nice bath. I took off my sports coat and draped it over my arm. A sports coat, you say? Maybe you find it hard to picture me in such a thing. I *always* wear a sports coat when out and about in Paris because Dr. Jonathan Newman had basically required it on our previous trips (*and* because I'm a gentleman, damn it!). It wasn't until we got off the train that I realized that my wallet, which I always kept in a pocket on the inside of my jacket—you can't be too careful about pickpockets, people!—had slipped out and was gone.

Losing your wallet anywhere, but especially in a foreign country, is always a nightmare. But somehow Steve and I had managed to make it worse. We had put our whole budget for the trip in my checking account before we left, planning to use my debit card to pay for things as we went. And because we aren't *idiots*, we also brought one of Steve's credit cards to use in case of emergency. Then we put both cards in my wallet. The missing one.

Now, the French get a lot of shit for being not particularly warm or friendly. And France, sweetheart, I would love to be able to defend your good name here—to describe in intimate but hilarious detail the number of Parisians who jumped at the chance to help us in this, our darkest hour of need. I wish I could say that a wizened old pensioner offered us a fresh baguette for *gratuit* or a handsome young poet swooped in to offer translation services or anything, but France, girl, I can't. And it hurts me to say this, because your capital city is genuinely beautiful, if bizarrely laid out, but unfortunately, the people of Paris were not only decidedly unhelpful, but some of them were also downright fucking rude. I hate to feed the stereotype, but it's true!

There was the man at the Metro station's literal "Help" window who slid the window shut In. Our. Faces. Then there was the cop who pretended not to speak English. And yes, I'm guessing that he was pretending, but let me tell you this: every single person I'd met in that town *in the five times I'd been there before* spoke English better than I did. Oh, those happy days with Dr. J when French people spoke English to us like we weren't some common American idiots! They were happy to speak it back when I was with my wealthy friend, when I had a wallet, and didn't even need their help. But now, a transit cop in one of the busiest Metro stops in the city can't speak English? I'm not buying it, Pierre.

And then, to add insult to injury, there was the *très chic* lady standing outside the Metro station, wearing sunglasses and smoking a cigarette—because of course. She had the cutest French bulldog—or, I guess, just "bulldog," as they would call them there?—I'd ever seen. In my very distressed state, wondering how difficult it would be to get a dishwashing job in Paris since we fucking lived there now, I thought at *least* I can get some small relief by giving this good little dog a scritch. Bending down to pet it, I looked over to the woman, made the petting motion with my hand and said, "Okay?" She took a long drag of her cigarette, blew all the smoke out through her nose like Satan, and then stuck one boney finger up and said, "Non." Which I didn't need a translator to understand was French for "Don't touch my fucking dog."

It's not big of me, but I have never forgotten or forgiven this woman who, in the many, many retellings of this story, I've come to call Marie An-TWAT-nette. It's a stretch and it's hard to say, but that's how strongly I feel about it. Aren't dog people supposed to be nice? Even French ones? My sister Sarah is a dog person, and when she calls me during her dogs' daily walks, I swear she's not calling to talk to me, but rather for me to hear her talk to *every other freaking dog person she encounters along her route.* I thought dog people were friendly! Too friendly! I don't even like dogs! I'm just having A Moment, you mean old French hag!

When we got back to the hotel, Steve called the credit card company and I called Citibank. I was more than welcome, I was told, to walk into any Citibank-affiliated bank to have my debit card replaced on the spot. Perfect! One small hiccup: the closest Citibank-affiliated bank was in Madrid. Madrid, Spain. A short 792 miles away. As I prepared to pitch myself off the cute Juliet balcony, Steve took the phone from me and was able to arrange for new cards to meet us in Barcelona, when we arrived there in two days.

Steve also had been smart enough to stash a hundred euros in cash in the hotel safe with our passports. Since our tickets to Barcelona were prepaid, we would just have to live on our cash through the weekend. Now, a lot of people would have seen this as an adventure: *We'll live like Parisian bohemians for the weekend, surviving on the cheap! We'll get baguettes and peasant cheese and the local winemaker's most primitive blend and picnic by the Seine . . .*

I promise you that is not how I handled it. I moped. I complained. I actually called the *US embassy* (?!) to see if they would float us some cash until we got this all sorted out. (Steve had to leave the room for that.) We spent the next two days walking around Paris drinking coffee, going to free museums. We spent a full rainy afternoon in a café writing postcards to our families. We wandered by the Eiffel Tower and took pictures—pictures where we look so *insanely* in love that they seem staged and that, as I write this, are framed and sitting on shelves in our living room all these years later. Sounds terrible, right? Of course it wasn't! It was great, maybe perfect! But I couldn't recognize that at the time. Instead, I was grumpy, and annoyed, and a general un-delight to be around! Have I mentioned that I'm a very, very young soul?

We finally made it to Barcelona on Monday morning, but the mail hadn't yet arrived at our hotel. Even though we were down to our last fifty euros, I was starving, so we ended up at a little sandwich shop across the street from our hotel. And it was at that little sandwich shop that everything changed.

We walked in, ordered our sandwiches from the handsome sandwich guy at the counter, and then scarfed them down at one of the tables. I was feeling better already—a lot less hangry and grateful for the bit of Spanish eye candy. Soon we'd have our debit card and be back on track with this terrible trip. Spain—not France—was where our trip was *really* going to start. When we got up to leave, I waved goodbye to the hot sandwich guy, tossed out an *"Adios y gracias"* like a real local, and then walked face-first, at what felt like a hundred miles an hour, into the closed glass door.

In case you're wondering, the crashing sound produced by the collision of a not-small gay human man and a not particularly sturdy or well-hung glass door is . . . loud. And to the credit of every human present, nobody laughed—which I actually found curious, because there is no question that what had just happened was absurdly hilarious. *I* would have laughed if I saw me wave at the hot sandwich guy, mumble some Spanish, and then hurl myself through a glass door like a fucking pigeon.

For me, everything went black for a second. I had fully expected to, you know, walk right through what appeared to me to be *open space*. Instead, the world stopped as my brain readjusted to reality: *Is there glass everywhere? Am I made of glass? Is this another dimension?* Once I recovered, I realized that I was completely fine, still here on Earth, in Barcelona, in a sandwich shop—just glass-covered and *very* embarrassed. Every one of the Catalonian faces stared at me with absolute pity. But not with the sweet, "Are you okay?" kind of pity—with the "Wow, Americans really are as stupid as I thought" kind. I pushed what was left of the door open, collapsed in *very* dramatic fashion onto a bench just outside, and burst into humiliated tears. Steve put his arm around me and just let me cry.

This trip had been a lot. I was frustrated and tired and I wasn't having any fun. But something else had been nagging at me—like *really* nagging at me. Steve and I had always prided ourselves on the fact that we didn't want kids. Remember how we'd made that joke that instead of having children, we'd just go on vacations and name them? The moment we made that joke—brilliant and hilarious as it was—a little voice in my head started asking if I meant it. And if I was honest with myself, I knew that I didn't. And maybe it was the exhaustion, or the head wound, or the condescending looks from the Barcelonians still staring at me from inside the restaurant, but something just bubbled up in me. Sitting there, sobbing on that bench, feeling vulnerable, I had a real moment of clarity: I wanted a fucking kid. I didn't want to name trips. I didn't want to be a First-Class Travel Gay. I didn't want to globe-trot around the world, smashing myself into other glass doors or losing my wallet in new, exotic cities. I wanted to belong somewhere and have someone belong to me. I didn't want to see the world; I wanted to build a world—build a family—with Steve.

"I want a fucking kid," I blurted out to Steve.

And as though he somehow had been reading my mind, he nodded his head and said, "Me too."

. . . .

I'm not what anyone would call a "dawdler," so as soon as we got home from our trip I began looking into our options. Neither Steve nor I have a uterus, so creating our own kid for "free" was off the table. If we wanted a kid, it was looking like we were going to have to spend some money.

The two most obvious real-world options were surrogacy or a traditional agency adoption. We quickly ruled out surrogacy for a couple of reasons. First of all, according to my research, surrogacy could cost anywhere from $90,000 to $130,000 or higher. Secondly, neither Steve nor I felt a particular need for our kid to share our DNA. It seemed to us that there were probably plenty of kids out there who needed a safe, loving home that we could provide, even if that meant depriving the world of yet another awkward-looking, chubby little Hinds baby. Unfortunately, though, traditional adoption also seemed out of reach for us, with a price tag of about $70,000. Oof. Like, excuse me, but fucking WHAT? Where is all that money going? Shouldn't we be _giving_ kids to qualified loving parents and then maybe using that sweet 70K to put them through college or something? BRB, going to tweet AOC about this.

Also, where are you gays who pick one of these two options getting all your money? We knew at least two other gay couples going through this at the same time as we were; both couples made less money than we did and still, somehow, went the swanky surrogacy route. Incidentally, one of these couples flatly refused to tell anyone which one of them would be the bio dad. But it became abundantly was funny in that self-deprecating way us gays love and was a native French speaker who, like him, loved a good afternoon tea. Cosette . . . he was less fond of. She was a twenty-three-year-old "former model" who still lived at home and seemed to have little motivation to get a job and/or move out. And forgive the bitchiness of the air quotes around "former model," but her entire modeling career had consisted of one photo shoot for Abercrombie & Fitch that never saw the light of day—MUCH to the chagrin of Fantine, who, it turned out, derived much of her own self-worth from other people finding her daughter attractive. Cosette, in return, seemed to resent her mother's attention and constant focus on her looks. And so the two women, who insisted they were *BEST FRIENDS!*, bickered constantly.

Dr. Jonathan Newman wasn't one for conflict. So now, staring down the barrel of a month in the rustic isolation of a provincial farmhouse with these two, he knew he needed a bit of upbeat backup to survive: me. Rosé and cheese in Provence, and all I had to do was run interference between my rich pal and his two French friends? Count me in.

A few weeks later, I landed at the Nice airport and hopped on a train to Provence. The train traveled along the Mediterranean coastline and then up through part of southern France's wine country. At the train station, I hopped in the car Dr. Jonathan Newman had sent for me, which whisked me off through a small downtown area to the outskirts of town, where, at the end of a long dirt road, I finally arrived at the "farmhouse."

I don't know what I was expecting—something rustic and, I don't know, a little bit weatherworn? A crumbling villa? Maybe a middle-class home that was part of a working farm or something? But that was not what I was looking at. This was . . . *spectacular:* one clear upon the child's birth that they had gone with the . . . smart dad over the hot dad. Interesting choice, fellas.

It's not that Steve and I were exactly *poor* at this stage in our lives. We were both working as concierges at separate upscale Manhattan hotels—jobs that paid surprisingly well. So we were doing fine—more than fine by many measures—but we just didn't have the equivalent of a house down payment burning a hole in our savings account. I mean, we *barely* had a savings account at all.

But there was also one other option: "foster to adopt." I'd been seeing signs for it all over the subway: beautiful pictures of children and families with the slogan "Be the reason." One ad said, "Be the reason he feels loved. Help an NYC child who needs a safe and loving home by becoming a Foster or Adoptive Parent." Another seemed directly aimed at couples like Steve and me: "Be the reason it gets better. Help an LGBTQ child by becoming an LGBTQ-affirming Foster or Adoptive Parent."

These ads spoke to us. We sort of felt called to the foster care system. There would always be people with means ready to adopt the kids being put up for traditional adoption; in fact, there are often way more families looking to adopt that way than there are kids available. I hoped we weren't being naive, but we wanted to be parents *now*, so why not dive into a system that desperately needed parents rather than getting on endless wait lists and hoping to someday, somehow get picked. Plus, with the foster care system, we had a chance to take in a kid who might otherwise be bounced from home to home until they were eighteen. It seemed like an opportunity to make a real difference. Something about it just felt right.

A few weeks later, we went to a foster parent orientation. This was an opportunity for the twenty or so state-run agencies to make a little presentation about who they are and why foster parents should consider working with them. Most of the other fifty or so prospective foster parents were retirement-aged women of color. Looking around the auditorium, I leaned over to Steve and said, "Where the hell are all the gays?"

"Happy hour," he said, dryly.

Attending this orientation was a big step for Steve. He wanted a kid as much as I did, but he just tends to, you know, think things through. Foster-to-adopt felt right for him too, but the one thing a more traditional adoption would have afforded us is time. Steve is a fan of time. And of planning. *I* do not suffer from the same sad and boring affliction of sweating the details. I'm *FUN!* and *SPONTANEOUS!* and always sure things will just work out! So while Steve was sitting there already thinking about how on *earth* we'd be able to change our erratic work schedules to actually care for this kid, which felt to him like it was going to come to us at any moment—hell, we might even leave with one in a to-go bag today—I was busy fantasizing about the fun stuff: baby Christmas outfits and birthday parties and, oh my God, should we maybe get a pony?!

When the orientation was over, attendees were invited to speak with the various agency representatives. We definitely wanted to talk with one of the only agencies that worked with newborn babies, but their name, Episcopal Social Services, gave us pause. I'm an on-the-record believer in God. But, sorry religious people, some of your institutions tend to be mean and scary for the gays—you know, the whole "God created Adam and Eve, not Patrick and Steve" thing.

Luckily, nobody threw holy water at us. Instead we were immediately put at ease by a young Latina woman named Luisa. Her whole vibe was welcoming and warm. Maybe it's cliché to say that she had a "kind face," but she did—with her big brown eyes and easy smile, she said a simple "Hello" and we knew we'd found our agency. Plus, it turned out that even though Episcopal Social Services had been founded by nuns in the 1800s, it no longer had any religious affiliation.

Luisa asked us to tell her about ourselves and why we wanted to be foster parents. When we told her that we were looking for a baby and were interested in adoption, she explained to us that the goal of foster care is always to reunite children with their birth parents: "There are some instances where reunification isn't possible and foster parents can pursue the path of adoption. But it's important to keep in mind that reunification with parents or another family member is always the goal."

Aha, I thought. Here was the catch. This foster-to-adopt system wasn't full of kids who had been pre-cleared for adoption and were looking for full-time permanent placements. These were kids who had been removed from their birth parents for any number of reasons, with the hope that the parents would someday be able to take them back. This was new information for us but made complete sense. For Steve and me, though, this was a big risk. It was possible—even probable—that we could be matched with a baby, raise it as our own for an unknown amount of time, and then have it taken away from us, never to be seen again. Maybe it was too big a risk.

But I'm a big believer in fate. One time my friend Colleen was headed to a birthday party for our friend Dawn. When Colleen got out of her taxi, she left Dawn's gift behind. Thirty minutes later, our friend Tom hailed a cab headed to the same party, and wouldn't you know it, when he climbed into the back seat, he found the gift Colleen had forgotten. New York City is a city of nine million people and nearly fifteen thousand taxis. I mean, what are the odds? So was it a coincidence, or did the universe just KNOW that Dawn couldn't live without that DVD box set of *Murder She Wrote*?

I believe the latter.

Steve thinks I'm ridiculous.

But as we sat there listening to beautiful Luisa tell us all the ways in which a foster-to-adopt plan could break our hearts, I *knew* that Steve and I were meant to be parents. That we were *going* to be parents. I didn't know *how* it would happen, but I knew that it *would* happen. And since this was the path right in front of us, it felt like the right way forward.

. . . .

The next step in the foster-to-adopt process was to complete a ten-week "Model Approach to Partnerships in Parenting (MAPP)" training course. This, I was excited for. It was my understanding that this was a "parenting basics" class where they taught you the important stuff like how to change a diaper. Or how to, you know, like, *feed* a baby. Or get a baby to sleep! How often are they supposed to sleep? And for how long? That would be good to know! And also: how to *hold* a baby because I feel like there is something you definitely have to do or definitely not do with the neck, right? And obviously, you have to burp a baby because . . . that's something you have to do sometimes, or else the baby dies? Oh! How not to kill a baby by accident—that would be an important thing to learn!

Some of you baby whisperers out there think I'm kidding, but all of the above were skills that somebody was going to have to teach me. At thirty-five years old, I didn't have a great track record when it came to caring for children. I had been left alone with a child exactly once, a few years before, when my sister Sarah desperately needed someone to watch her six-month-old son one morning. I remember her placing the sleeping baby in my arms before walking out the door at 6 AM. He was quiet and perfect and—I swear to God—*cooing*, until he heard the door close. Then that little fucker's eyes popped open like the Chucky doll from that horror movie, except meaner, and he screamed like a scared rabbit for the rest of the day. I dare you to YouTube what a screaming rabbit sounds like. You will not be okay. Needless to say, when my sister called to check on me at 10 AM, four short hours later, I was exhausted and sobbing and begged her to come home. I was not strong.

But this class was going to set me straight and give me all the skills I'd need to keep a kid alive!

Or . . . not.

Within minutes of our first class, it became clear that it was not going to be the "basics" class that I'd thought it would be. Beautiful Luisa, our teacher, passed around a syllabus for the ten weeks. Topics included "Emotional Maturity," "Conflict De-escalation with Adolescents," and "Discipline in the Foster Home."

"WHAT?" I scream-whispered to Steve. "Where are the units on changing a shitty DIAPER? I don't know how to do that! WHEN ARE THEY GONNA TEACH US HOW TO DO THAT?"

SHUT UP!! Steve wrote at the top of his paper. Two exclamation marks; he was fucking serious. He was already going through the packet underlining things. He didn't care what this class taught; he was just glad to be back in a classroom—a place where he knows he's better than everyone. I could already see him hoping for a test. Honestly, I really don't recommend taking a class with your spouse; it brings out an ugly side of them. We came in as a couple and soon enough, Steve would be hanging out with the honors kids and abandoning me with the other underachieving weirdos and freaks who didn't know how to diaper.

The ten-week class flew by. Even though it was packed with information that didn't really apply to us—it was mostly about handling the social and emotional issues when fostering a teenager who'd been in the system for years—Steve and I really looked forward to the weekly sessions. It was fun to be around other people experiencing the same sort of parental anticipation as we were. None of us knew for sure the kind of kid we were going to be matched with, but we all knew that no matter what, they'd be coming from some sort of difficult circumstance and that we might be the first stabilizing force they would know. That's a pretty serious responsibility, and we loved being around other people who also felt a calling to be that kind of positive presence.

The rest of the process went surprisingly fast. After home inspections and background checks, we completed the final paperwork to receive our official foster-parent licenses. I hand delivered our packet to the agency on my way to work at the Midtown hotel where I was a concierge. And bam. We were now ready to be parents, apparently.

About forty-five minutes later, I was at the front desk, refilling the double-decker bus maps and directions to the Empire State Building when my phone vibrated. It was the foster care agency. I answered it quickly.

"Patrick, it's Luisa. We have a baby for you."

"Wait, what?? WHAT??" I shouted, as I ran from the desk, through the back door and into the back hallway. "You have a baby?"

"She came into the system today. We don't have a lot of information right this minute, but she's six days old, she's healthy, and she needs a placement starting today. Will you guys take her?"

This was insane. Even though we'd been clear with our agency that we wanted to foster a baby that had a high likelihood of eventually being cleared for adoption, we'd been told that we'd need to be patient. They told us repeatedly that it might take *years*. Not forty-five minutes.

"I have to call Steve," I said. I was shaking from head to toe.

"Okay," she said. "But the agency closes at five and we have to place her before then. You guys were my first call, so let me know ASAP."

I know we're right in the middle of the whole reason you wanted to read this chapter in the first place—the big dramatic baby moment—but I just gotta take a quick second to say that amidst all the insanity that was about to be my next twenty-four hours, this moment has always stood out to me. Like, did Luisa really say they had to place this baby before quitting time (?!) at 5 PM? And if they didn't, then what? If there was ever a reason for someone to put in a little bit of overtime, shouldn't this be it? Not only were they asking us to make the most important decision of our lives, but like what was going to happen to the baby if we called back at 5:01? Was it getting stuffed in a file cabinet until morning? *Hank, just file this one under "M for Morning Babies." I gotta catch my bus. Ya know what, just toss a bottle in there to be safe. Goo-goo, baby. Okay, I'm off!*

Anyway, I was not looking forward to this phone call with Steve. He'd gone back to school to get the math degree he'd always wanted (kids, listen to your parents: that theater degree really is useless), and was actually in class at that very moment. It was March. We'd decided that we'd wait until June, when Steve's classes would be done for the semester, to officially "open our home" for a placement from the agency. This was the plan. Steve likes plans. Steve does not like when plans change.

I called. No answer.

I called again. No answer. It was 4:34. I wondered, probably aloud, if it was *for sure* wrong for me to just go ahead and make this decision without him. I mean, he'd be okay with it *eventually*, right? But also, one time I impulse bought a rug for our entryway without Steve, and he glared at me for a week. And this was a *baby*.

My phone buzzed. It was him.

"Babe," I said. "Luisa called. They have a baby for us."

"What?" he said. "Oh my God."

This wasn't a "no." Which I knew meant I could get him to "yes." I just had to work fast. "We don't know a lot, but she's healthy and they need to place her tonight."

"TONIGHT?" he screamed. "Or what?"

"Or I think they kill her."

Steve scream-laughed. "Oh God. You're not getting off the phone until I say yes, are you?"

"I'm not."

"Well then, I guess it's decided," he said.

"No, you have to say it."

"Say what?"

"You have to *say* yes."

There was about three seconds of silence, and then a deep breath, and then "Yes."

. . . .

I ran into my boss's office. She'd heard the whole conversation. She pulled me into a quick hug and then shouted, "GO! Go meet your baby!" I grabbed my things and ran out the door, headed to the subway. On the way, I called my sister Sarah. For the last ten weeks, since we'd started our MAPP classes, every time I called her, she'd answer the phone with "OH MY GOD IS IT HAPPENING? IS A BABY COMING???" And I'd have to remind her of the timeline.

This time, when the baby *actually was coming*, she didn't answer.

"SARAH!" I screamed into her voicemail, "THIS. IS. THE. CALL. CALL ME BACK. THE BABY IS COMING!" I heard myself say it out loud for the first time, and—say it with me—I burst into hysterical tears.

I got home a little after 5:30. The baby could be arriving at any moment. I looked around our apartment and saw it for what it was: a filthy baby death trap. *Oh my God*, I thought, *would the agency people change their minds?* I jumped into action: covering outlets, cleaning the kitchen, scrubbing the bathroom—*Jesus Christ how had we let our bathroom get so grimy? We are SUCH BAD GAAAAAAAAAAAAAAYS.*

After all that, the baby didn't end up coming that night. I literally took to the bed at six o'clock when the agency called to say they'd make the delivery—the words they actually used—the next afternoon. No, they assured us, she was not being kept in a file cabinet, which was all I could imagine as it quickly became clear that I was going to be the kind of parent who could only imagine the worst-case scenario. It quickly became clear to *me*, I should clarify; everyone else in my life already knew I'd be a wreck.

In the morning, Steve left for class, planning to be back before afternoon. Why was he acting like this was just another normal day? Was this some kind of elaborate prank? Was this baby coming at all? I was about to get up, make coffee, and settle in for a long day of moping when I heard a car pull up outside our apartment. *Could it be?* I wondered.

A blue minivan was double-parked in front of the building. A woman got out and opened the long sliding door to the back seat.

My heart was pounding. I don't know what I expected the baby delivery to be like, but this seemed too casual. Shouldn't there be some kind of official-looking vehicle? Was this a minivan full of babies that they just drove around all day like some kind of pizza delivery service? Baby Grubhub? Joe's Pizza and Baby Delivery?

Luckily, I had the presence of mind to snap a picture as the woman pulled the baby carrier from the back seat. Though we didn't have a picture of our baby in the delivery room when she was born, this is the picture that I show people: an open minivan and a baby in a car seat being hefted out onto a New York City street. The moment she was brought into our lives.

A minute later, there was a knock on my door. When I opened it, there was a young, pretty, official-looking woman standing there with the baby carrier. "I'm Charmane with Administrative Children's Services," she said. "Can I come in?"

"Of course," I said nervously.

She handed me the baby carrier as she passed me in the hallway. This woman was not fucking around.

"Can I take your coat?" I asked.

"No," she said. "I won't be staying long." She gave me a paper bag containing pre-made bottles of formula. "You'll want to feed her every four hours. Do you have clothes for her? This is all she has."

She held up a onesie the nurses at Beth Israel hospital had given her. Across the front, it said, "I'm a BI baby." Charmane didn't seem in the mood to joke around, so I tucked away the bisexual baby joke for another time.

"The agency will call you later with more details," Charmane said as she headed for the door. *Gotta get all those babies delivered before 5 PM*, I thought.

I looked down at the little creature sound asleep under a blanket in the carrier. She was so tiny, so *hairy*, so so perfect.

Charmane was halfway out the door when I yelled, "Wait! What's her name?"

"Oh right," Charmane said with a smile. "This is Daisy."

Chapter Eight

WHY THE FUCK DID I OPEN A DAYCARE?

Daisy's arrival upended everything in our lives in the best possible way. With our erratic work and school schedules, it had been years since Steve and I had a full day off together. Sometimes he'd be working an overnight shift at his job and I'd be on the morning shift at mine; we could go days without actually seeing each other. But the new baby changed all of that. We both took several weeks' leave from our jobs, Steve finished up school, and the three of us just nested. Going back to work after that was really, really hard. Luckily, though, I'd known that the second I met our future kid, I would never want to leave them, so I had already hatched a plan. A plan that made perfect sense to me. A foolproof plan that *could not* fail. I was going to open a home daycare.

Hold for applause.

In my defense, this was not a totally impulsive decision. At that point, I'd lived in New York for fifteen years. I'd spent the first ten of those bartending and then another five working as a hotel concierge. These were not easy jobs. Basically, I'd had fifteen years of enduring drunk and entitled New York City tourists, aka dealing with the absolute worst of humanity. I was ready for a change of pace. I was tired of coddling the needy, demanding, and rude. I was ready to start working with toddlers.

Yes, yes, in retrospect I know it seems crazy that I thought I could be successful at running a daycare. But at the time, I was sure it was going to work. It's true that I don't particularly like children who aren't Daisy, and yes, I have absolutely no patience. But I can be good with kids! I mean, I'm good with my kid, right? It couldn't be that different looking after other people's kids, could it?

Having seen a few home daycares, it seemed like the greatest idea ever. My older sister's friend had a home daycare in the suburbs outside Boston, and I'd seen how easy it was. She had a few sweet little kids, they played some games, she took them for a walk, they'd have a nap—bada-bing, bada-boom, it's happy hour! It was a no-brainer. Plus, I'd get to work from home, be with my kid all day, and be my own boss. For a year, as I waited to put my home daycare into action, Steve had been the primary dad and I was never really there; I really looked forward to finally spending more quality time with my child.

Also, I'm not gonna lie: it seemed like a gold mine. Daycares in my area were charging $325 per week for full-time care. I did the math: if I hired one full-time person (at, say, $12 per hour), the state regulations said that we could take up to six kids. So that's $325 per week per kid minus one kid for Daisy minus $12 per hour, times . . . well, more like I *tried* to do the math. But whatever, it sounded like a lot.

Notice you don't hear me saying that I wanted to enrich the lives of children, or that I really had this calling to teach children about the world. My reasons for opening the daycare were all very selfish. But that's capitalism, baby! Playing with kids and raking in the dough. Why wasn't everyone opening daycares in their homes? It was a sure thing. *Not* opening a daycare was for suckers.

But I wanted to do it right. For once in my life, I wasn't going to rush. I knew it might take some time to figure everything out, and I wanted to be as prepared and ready to go as possible before I launched. I was going to need, like, permits or something? Right? Maybe a . . . license? Oh, and some idea of what to do with a bunch of kids all day—that'd be helpful! In short, what I needed was *experience*—to get my hands dirty. Luckily, I knew exactly who I needed to call: Fremme Drag Mom.

For years, Steve and I had lived in an apartment building way uptown. The neighborhood was a cool combination of Dominican families, Orthodox Jewish families, and a sprinkling of hot young gays. Even though we didn't live there anymore, we still had a friend in the building—a young Orthodox Jewish woman—who'd been running a home daycare for years. She was in her late twenties and had two young kids and a ridiculously hot—and embarrassingly timid—husband named Levi. Her name was Fremme, and because she was just super cool and kind to everyone in the building, all the building-gays called her "Fremme Drag Mom," or FDM. (If you've never watched *RuPaul's Drag Race*, Drag Mothers are basically boss bitches with BDE: Big Drag [Queen] Energy. They're motherly and loving, but they don't take any shit and they always tell it like it is.) Levi didn't stand a chance around FDM. All the building-gays were obsessed with her.

So, I called FDM and told her about my plan to open a home day-care. When I asked if I could come train with her a few days a week, she didn't hesitate: "Absolutely fucking yes." I was relieved, and not just because I knew that learning the ropes from Fremme would be both fun *and* educational. Something to note here that the heterosexuals among you (Hey, Derek!) might not know: gays of a certain age—my age—have been conditioned to think we'll be seen as creepy child molesters if we express the *slightest* interest in hanging out with kids who aren't our own. So, I wasn't sure that I'd be given a chance. In fact, on the first day working for Fremme, some parents definitely gave me some sideways glances. But I didn't think it would be that helpful for me to say, "Hi, I'm Patrick. I'm Fremme's new assistant, and I swear to God I'm into grown-ups *only!*"

The parents came around surprisingly quick. Mostly because parents are assholes who are very glad to make their children your problem for the day. And I could definitely understand why they didn't want to be around some of these kids. As an example, there was this one five-year-old who would come in every day guzzling a thermos of chocolate milk. As a chocolate milk lover myself, I get it. But every day, within five minutes of drop-off, he would completely, epically, shit his pants. We begged the mother to switch to water or juice or fucking vodka—*anything*. But it didn't bother her because from 8 AM onwards, Choco-Shitter was our problem.

And then there was the one kid who was always breaking things with his incredible strength. One time, while most of the kids colored in their little Jewish folktale coloring books, he hulked out and slammed some French doors, shattering three of the panes. No wonder his parents didn't want him at home.

Luckily, FDM was great at her job—a true inspiration to all aspiring caregivers. I had a lot to learn from her. She was very sweet with the kids (which I was good at), but also firm (which . . . not so much). I once let myself get hit in the face with a swing in order to snap Daisy out of a tantrum on the playground. She instantly stopped crying and started laughing and begging me to do it again. My lip was bleeding, but even still, I considered it. See! I'm fun! And kind! The kids at *my* daycare would do what I asked because they would love and respect me. I didn't need to learn firmness.

I only saw Fremme frazzle once. On Fridays, we baked challah bread with the kids—it was a Fremme Drag Mom daycare tradition I'd come to love. On this particular Friday, Fremme wasn't feeling that great, we had challah in the oven, and Choco-Shitter had had a stealth second shit. As I was changing his diaper, I somehow smelled not choco poo but smoke. *Oh no*, I thought, *the bread was burning in the oven.* I realized that FDM was in the bathroom, presumably puking from the smell of Choco-Shitter's unending anal tidal wave of human waste. All the kids started screaming, and FDM came running in to make sure we didn't all die.

Now, like most Orthodox women, FDM always wore a headscarf because—as she had explained to me with an epic eye roll—a woman does not show her hair after her wedding, because her hair is a sexy thing that is just for hot, shy Levi or something. I probably have that wrong. But as she rescued us, her headscarf started falling off, and, rather than scrambling to fix it, she yelled, "Oh fuck it, you're gay, they're children, and it's too damn hot in here for this crap," as she flung the headscarf into the corner. *That's* Big Drag Queen Energy.

Being with the kids, changing diapers, seeing how to save kids from burning to death in a fire: priceless. There's really nothing like hands-on experience. Except that I should be clear that the "few days a week" I worked for FDM were specifically *two* days a week—and those two days were half days. So, two full half days—8 AM to 11 AM.

Also, from 10 to 11, she had me running errands. Boss lady had a lot of dry cleaning that needed picking up. You wouldn't think you'd need to dress so well to work with kids, but here we are. So, maybe that full year of working four hours a week at someone else's home daycare wasn't total preparation for becoming a full-time childcare giver and business owner. But it was a start.

Learning complete, we had to get our home ready. At the time, we lived in a two-bedroom apartment in Harlem. There might've been something in our lease about not being allowed to start a business in our apartment, but I'd also read online that there was a loophole for home daycares? Maybe? It seemed like a "beg forgiveness, not ask permission" situation if it ever came to it, right? The most important thing was to clear out anything that read "Grown-ups live here" and replace it with welcoming kid stuff. The plan was for me and Steve to keep our bedroom largely intact, but to turn the living room and Daisy's room into a (cue music) *haven of fun and learning for children!*

Even though Steve and I aren't "stuff" people, it wasn't easy seeing all the vestiges of our adult human existence carted off to be replaced by cheerful alphabet letters and zoo animal murals. When these two guys from Craigslist came over to take our couch, one of them must have seen the fear in my eyes. On the way out he asked, "Hey—are you sure about this?"

But like any good hostage in the early stages of Stockholm syndrome, I yelped a high-pitched "YUP!"

Then came the cubbies, cots, craft tables, and colorful, child-friendly carpets as we laid out the few thousand dollars we had on transforming our home into the most cheerful fucking place you've ever seen. We spent days strategizing Circle Time activities under the watchful gaze of the monkeys in our murals. Did I detect a bit of skepticism in their googly eyes? How dare they judge us. We were taking a leap into the unknown, but also building our future. I'd done the work and was about to reap the rewards. So what if these crazed-looking monkeys would be the first thing I saw in the morning and the last thing I saw before bed? The kids would love them.

I put in my two weeks' notice at the hotel and prepared for the opening with Steve. It had never been the plan to have Steve work at the daycare, but it just kind of happened. Finding someone willing to work as a daycare assistant for twelve dollars an hour wasn't as easy as I'd expected, plus Steve had just finished his math degree and had quit his hotel job to look for a, like, math job(??), and by some miracle he hadn't found one yet. (Honestly, what even *is* a math job?) So, it all aligned that he was either serendipitously free to help me or maybe he just had a sense of where this was all going and didn't want to miss the show. But whatever the case was, thank fucking God he was available. So, with both of us working full-time at the daycare, we ended up just hiring our local babysitter to work part-time, along with my friend Claire, who agreed to work a bit in exchange for free full-time daycare for her son. Plenty of fun adults on hand for the kids.

Kids! We needed kids. Now, if you're in the daycare game, you know that ideally you get a bunch of kids around the same age. That way they make good playmates, they eat at the same time, nap at the same time, and, like, understand the same arts and crafts assignment objectives. Two to four years old is the sweet spot. The main thing is: NO BABIES. Babies are the fucking worst for a daycare. They're unpredictable, loud, don't give a fuck about the jungle murals you busted your ass on, and are constantly, *constantly*, c o n s t a n t l y shitting. I'd had enough of shitting.

And you want full time. None of this part-time, dribs and drabs, piecemeal stuff. Full time is where the money's at. If you really wanna rake it in, you need six kids whose parents barely want to see them. Six kids—two- to four-year-olds, hopefully—full time, loving those monkey decals, and not shitting.

Understandably, not every parent is willing to take a chance on a new daycare. But we hoped there'd be enough desperate, perhaps lazy, parents who were willing to take a gamble on us. Though maybe I should have taken it as a bad sign when our neighbors from across the street—our best parent friends, who were *constantly* complaining about how far away their current daycare was—didn't put their kid in *our* daycare.

"Oh . . . um, you know, Sam isn't really good with change," his mother nervously told me.

"Well, think about it!" I said, cheerfully. "We're right there! Hamilton Heights Daycare! Wow, that rhymes!"

I was trying to seem pleasant and not desperate. I didn't want to spook her, and I could only bring it up so many times without setting off pedo alarm bells. But this was crazy! Sam was *perfect*: two and a half years old, with his best daycare years ahead of him. A walking (well, toddling) daycare gold mine!

But it wasn't to be. Instead, in addition to Daisy, our perfect one-and-a-half-year-old, we ended up with a grab bag of neighborhood kids, all different ages and styles. A veritable B-Team of unwanted children whose parents happened to live nearby:

There was Emma, just a year old, but the size of a three-year-old. This kid was huge. Just thick and solid and tall. A log of a kid. Her parents seemed to be in denial about her size; she always came jammed into clothes that were appropriate for her age but not her girth. And they were for sure trying to shrink her, because they had her on a diet that . . . seemed to not work for her insides. She was too young, and a shitter. Strike one.

Then there was Oliver, a two-year-old, who looked exactly like Apple Inc. cofounder Steve Wozniak. You know, the Woz. Now before you start calling me a nerd, consider that I only know who the Woz is because he briefly dated comedian and bitchy gay icon Kathy Griffin. So, in case you are neither a nerd nor a homosexual, and you don't know what Steve Wozniak looks like, he can best be described as a cross between an Ewok and a pillow. Seriously, do an image search. You can't unsee it. And Oliver was his spitting image. Anyway, Oliver would scream and cry from the moment his mother left him until the moment she picked him up. Truly, it was like nothing I'd ever seen. On the second day Oliver was with us, fifteen minutes into his regular tantrum, I told Steve, who was pulling out every childcare trick in the book to calm the tantrum, that I was going to call Oliver's mother to come pick him up.

"For crying? At a daycare?" Steve asked, looking up from the basket of musical toys he was waving in Oliver's face.

"Yes?" I answered. What was Steve not understanding here? This kid was killing the vibe!

I decided to tough it out until the end of the day. I wanted to be responsible, so at pickup I started explaining to Oliver's mother that he'd basically cried all day. She seemed pretty unfazed by it.

Trying to be helpful and to show my commitment to little Oliver's good time, I said, "Well, I'll spend some time tonight Googling what to do about it," I said.

This stopped the mother dead in her tracks. "You're going to . . . Google how to handle a crying kid?"

"Yeah," I reassured her, "I'll Google!"

Little Woz never came back.

And then there was Charlotte. As a four-year-old, she should have been my favorite, my moneymaker. Instead, she was my nemesis. To understand how this happened, you have to understand that to run a daycare, you need a routine—a *schedule*—to ensure everything goes smoothly. With a proper plan in place, your day will go off without a hitch. So, we had it all mapped out:

7 AM–8 AM: Children arrive! Free play time!

I shit you not, I imagined playing classical music while the younger children, I don't know, cooed and rolled around on the floor. The older children would be drawn to the reading nook and curl up on a beanbag chair (note to self: don't forget to get a reading nook and a beanbag chair). Some of the artsier kids would color and craft or work on their independent projects because the environment we'd created had them so self-motivated to *create*. Meanwhile, I'd stand by the door while the parents showered me in compliments about how beautiful the space was ("Thank you, I *did* paint that monkey mural!"), and what a *godsend* the daycare was ("I do it for the *children*"), and how they literally could not remember how they ever survived without us ("I *should* raise my rates? Thank you for saying that!"). I imagined that at the coffee station—soon to be set up, I assure you—parents could grab a cup to go on the way out the door to their *busy, important* lives. ("Yes, we *do* grind our own beans. You're right, no other daycare offers that!") We were going to be premium fucking caretakers.

8 AM–8:30 AM: Breakfast!

At Hamilton Heights Daycare, we only feed your kids *organic*. I'm talking berries at breakfast. Avo-fucking-cado for snack. Your kid doesn't like avocado? *Not yet*, they don't. But they will. And for lunch: even more healthy stuff. Apple slices. Grapes! . . . Other stuff! Just . . . a lot of healthy, organic shit.

At the very first snack time, of the very first day, the kids full-on refused to eat what they were given. They turned the avocado slices into disgusting little missiles that they threw at each other. Grapes were smashed underfoot like I had opened a baby vineyard. But no one was eating a thing. After the kids were done with their little food fight, Steve and I scrambled to find something they would eat so they wouldn't devolve into hangry little monsters later. Luckily, we had the opposite of avocados: knockoff Eggo waffles and syrup. This, they loved.

9 AM–11 AM: Playground time!

Since everything else was *so well structured* inside the daycare and there would be *so much learning*, playground time would be a chance for the kids to run free and blow off some steam! You know: relax and just be kids! Then back to the daycare for some more great learning and structure.

In reality, by day two we were spending the entire day at the playground except for eating and napping (NAPPING! Ha ha ha . . .) because I had no idea what to do with these kids. After the last kid was dropped off, I'd drag our huge, four-seat stroller down the stairs to the sidewalk. This thing was the size of a refrigerator and weighed a hundred pounds, and it took up the entire sidewalk, forcing people into the street to get past us. But it was a true lifesaver, because stroller time was the only time that the kids were actually quiet and content. Sometimes I would just circle the block a few times to enjoy the serenity. With the kids finally drowsy, finally not crying, and finally not shitting, I could bulldoze people into traffic and escape into my thoughts. *God*, I thought, *what have I done?*

11:30 AM–12 PM: Lunch!

Organic avocado! Sunflower butter on toast! Organic grilled chicken tenders! Nope, more not-quite-Eggo fucking waffles.

12 PM–2 PM: Naptime!

We'd read the kids a story or two while they got all snuggly on their little cots. We'd quietly draw the blinds, turn down the Brahms concertos, and let the little ones drift off to sleep to recharge. Then it would be me time. I'd make some coffee, maybe listen to a podcast, clean up a little—just tidying really, since the kids had already cleaned up after themselves so well, bless them. A few hours later, the little angels would wake up refreshed and ready for some stimulating afternoon activities.

Unfortunately, I never did get that me time. None of these little motherfuckers ever napped. Not once. Were they not worn out by the long stroller ride? Was it the store-brand Eggo waffles and half cup of syrup they ate minutes before we turned off the lights? Who's to say, really? I was a premium caregiver, not a nutritionist.

2 PM–3 PM: Wake up! Circle time!

The children would adorably rustle awake. Wiping the sleep from their cute little eyes, they'd gather into a circle for singing! *The wheels on the bus go round and round, round and round . . .* Then we'd count! Now let's practice the days of the week! But how the hell can you wake up if you never sleep? Answer me that, you maniacs!

3 PM–4 PM: Activities!

Okay, so maybe everything up to now was a debacle. But this is where we gays were really going to shine. Sure, a lot of daycares would probably spend time helping the children learn how to write their names. And yes, learning about how to express emotions through drawing and coloring, naturally. But hold on to your fucking hats, because at Hamilton Heights Daycare we did all that and more because we were a *theater-gay* daycare. It's a *gaycare*! Yes, that's right: this daycare would be all about dress-up. Welcome, my children, to the fabulous "costume corner" where kids could pick from an extensive collection of scarves, hats, and outfits to find a costume that expressed how they were feeling. Perhaps a boa for you, Oliver? Oh, I see by your pirate hat that you are feeling extra adventurous, Emma. Of course I'll dress up too! *What fun!* Yup, we'd be that drama club daycare where kids would discover themselves through Theater and Imaginative Play.

But when you haven't eaten all day, haven't had a moment to yourself, haven't even been able to listen to a *podcast*, you're basically in survival mode. That's why I closed the costume corner, said "Screw it," and hauled everyone back to the playground, rather than let them tear apart our apartment and strew beads everywhere.

4 PM–5 PM: Free time and pickup!

Again, after so much structure and learning, it's always nice to have a little free time at the end of the day. Plus, parents would be picking up at 5 PM, sharp, so you don't want to get started on some big project that has to be interrupted. But in reality, most parents didn't get there until 5:45 PM or well after 6 PM, seriously cutting into my me time.

So that was the schedule. And four-year-old Charlotte was my nemesis because she saw that this was all bullshit. She knew I was a fraud. She was wise beyond her years in a totally unhelpful way. Maybe it was my fault for trying too hard to impress her—her mother had made it clear that Charlotte's three-year-old sister (gold mine!) was up for grabs if things went well with Charlotte. I felt Charlotte's eyes on me all day, auditioning me.

She wasn't impressed. This kid had been around the daycare block. At lunch, she pointed out that the milk wasn't organic. *FUCK,* I thought, *I'm blowing it.* Then at nap time, I realized that I'd forgotten to tell families to bring their own sheet and blanket from home. Charlotte just smiled while I scrambled around trying to scrounge up blankets from our bedroom. Then she tossed and turned, whining that she was uncomfortable so loudly that it kept everyone else awake. During free play, she flew off the handle, raging about the lack of glitter. When I apologized profusely, explaining that we didn't have any today, but maybe we could get some for tomorrow, her face perked up slightly. With genuine hope in her voice, she turned to me and asked, "Are there going to be better adults tomor-row too?"

Probably not, Charlotte, probably not.

That was day one. On the morning of day two, Steve and I sat on the living room floor where the couch had once been, sipping coffee. It was almost 7 AM. *How were we going to do this again?*

"Charlotte is an asshole," I said. "She has to go."

Steve didn't even respond. *Unbelievable,* I thought. *He's on her side.*

The saving grace was that this was the day that my friend Claire was arriving from LA with her son Leo. She was the one who was going to work for us a few hours a week in exchange for free full-time daycare. Not only was she going to be welcome support, but hope-fully the addition of Leo would help improve the seriously uncool mix of kids in our group. Leo had a big, sunny personality and he was four. *You're not the only four-year-old now, Charlotte!*

By the time they arrived, we were already several hours into "play-ground time."

"Which one is Charlotte?" Claire asked.

I pointed her out. "She's the one doing the chalk drawing."

Claire took one look at her and said, "Oh shit, she sucks." Claire was ride or die. It was gonna be a good day.

Leo had to go to the bathroom but said he could hold it when he realized his only option was the filthy, doorless public restroom at the playground. Eventually we loaded the kids into the stroller and headed home. It was only a fifteen-minute walk or so, but by now it was clear that Leo really had to go, so we sped up our walking. We pulled up in front of the apartment building and started unloading the kids when total chaos ensued. One kid refused to get out of the stroller, another one was heading out into the street—Claire dashed after that one—and my own daughter was suddenly sobbing for no reason. Then I heard "OH MY GOD OH MY GOD!" behind me, and I just knew that Claire had chased a kid into the street where he had been hit by a fucking car. But nope. Claire was screaming because Leo had pulled down his shorts, bent over, and was now shitting onto a tree directly in front of our building. He wasn't even squatting; he was in full yoga tabletop pose. As Claire scooped him up and ran into the apartment, Charlotte just shook her head in disgust and disappointment. "Someone is going to have to clean that up," she said.

By day three, I was looking for an exit strategy. But if I gave up the daycare, what would we do? Steve didn't have a job yet, so we'd be living off our meager savings. And even then, you can take the children out of the home daycare, but you can't take the home daycare out of the home. As in, for the foreseeable future, we'd be living in a furniture-less, number/letter-lousy apartment with no couch and monkey decals. Even for Gays with No Taste™ like us, this was too tragic. Could I call the Craigslist guy back and say that I'd changed my mind?

And then it rained. My "spend the whole day at the playground" strategy was off the table. By two o'clock, the children, hopped-up on discount waffles and stir-crazy from a lack of structure, were working my last nerve. I checked to see if it was still raining. It was. *How could this be happening to me?* I'd spent a year of my life preparing to open this daycare. I'd gotten permits, shelled out money for monkey murals. I'd trained with Fremme Drag Mom, learning about dry-cleaning and not burning children. I thought I had it all figured out.

I'd had such vivid fantasies about what this would become. Sure, this first location—our living room—was modest. But what with all the lucrative four-year-olds clamoring to join our inventive and wonderful daycare, we'd be forced to expand. Soon we'd open a second location and a third. I'd imagined the profile headline in *New York* magazine:

DAYCARE KING OF NORTHERN MANHATTAN

with an incredibly flattering photo of me and like a million happy kids. Maybe a better title would be

THE CHILDCARE WHISPERER

because I'd be so in the childcare know that parents would come to me, seeking my advice on which kindergarten might best suit their individual child's temperament. By expanding my daycare empire and doling out my childcare wisdom, I'd steadily acquire soft power. I'm not saying that this would lead to me *definitely* running for city council, but I'd at least consider it when slews of parents inevitably demanded it.

Instead, it was 2 PM on day fucking three of this thing I'd worked so hard for, and the rain was pushing me over the edge. This daycare was supposed to be my future. It was supposed to be my identity! Charlotte was right; I was a glitterless fraud. Also, I hated it. Even if I could figure out a way to make it work, there was absolutely no way I could force myself to do this for the rest of my life. But what then? I couldn't go back to working in hotels. *Remember the time that bitch Cloris Leachman made you cry because you couldn't get her into the Waverly Inn for dinner?* You can't go back to that.

Suddenly, I couldn't breathe. I felt very, very hot. My heart was racing, and my legs were shaking. Was I having a panic attack? I ran through the living room, past Steve and Claire, over the screaming and pooping kids, and into the bedroom. I curled up into a fetal position on the bed.

After a minute of this not helping, I flew back past Steve and Claire, and all the screamers and poopers, to the kitchen. It felt like a million degrees in there. And yes, I know how fucking gay and dramatic this will sound, but I did the only thing I could think of: I opened the freezer, pushed the bottles of vodka aside, and stuck my head in. I stood there with my head in the freezer for several minutes. Even if it wasn't helping much, it was a good reminder that we still had vodka.

That night, I pulled the plug. It was time to face the music. The daycare had been a mistake, and it wasn't fair to me, or the kids, to continue to pretend it wasn't. With Steve's support, I composed an email to the parents of the children of Hamilton Heights Daycare to let them know the hard truth. It turned out, unfortunately, that our building was shutting us down. Yes, sadly, our insurance company only covered us for accidents inside the daycare and outside in public places like playgrounds. And it definitely did *not* cover any accidents occurring in the stairwell and hallways, which like, okay, but how are we going to even operate then? What would happen if Charlotte, in a fit of anger, pushed a kid down the stairs? The building would be liable. So, unfortunately, they were shutting us down. Yes, it was outrageous, and we could, of course, fight this injustice, but it would be a costly and lengthy process. So, while we considered our options, unfortunately the daycare would be closing. Friday would be our last (half) day.

We had opened on Monday. I wrote this email on Wednesday. We were closing on Friday. Hamilton Heights Daycare was open for only a week. And of course, the email was total bullshit. I came up with the whole story myself. Sometimes I wonder if I'm actually a serial killer.

On that Friday, the parents of Emma—the world's biggest one-year-old—handed me a card. Inside was a check for $200—an incredibly sweet parting gift of a tip. The hot dad gave me a hug and said, "Good luck, man. You built a really great thing here; I'm sure you're sad to see it end." Not really, Emma's hot dad. Not really.

Chapter Nine

IF AT FIRST YOU DON'T SUCCEED, FAIL, FAIL AGAIN

I don't mean to sound heartless, but the goodbyes to the parents and the kids on that last day of the daycare were . . . exhausting. Pretending I'd miss the kids, pretending I knew the parents' names, pretending I wasn't counting the seconds until they were all out of my apartment—and my life—so I could tear into that freezer vodka. I was literally living a lie and I was *done*.

The final parent to pick up was a single mom named Katrina, an attorney who always arrived frazzled and looking exhausted. On Monday, day one of the daycare, I'd pitied her.

"It feels like Katrina really hates her job," I'd remarked to Steve. "It just makes me feel so lucky to finally get to do the thing I was born to do."

"Uh-huh," Steve responded, as he ripped a metal fork out of the hand of a two-year-old toddling right past me en route to an open wall socket.

By Friday, I was Katrina—barely standing by the time she arrived to pick up her daughter Audra . . . er, Andrea?

"Why don't you grab a copy of your lease," she said to me, as she gathered her daughter's things. "Let me take a look and see if I can find you a loophole to keep this place going."

Steve and I froze, having the same thought: Was she onto us? She was the only parent who hadn't responded to our email. Had she been doing, like, lawyer shit behind the scenes to find out if we were lying? Despite having basically no issue with lying to anyone about anything, I have a deep and abiding fear of getting into trouble or being yelled at. Oh no, was she about to yell at us? Or worse, was she GOING TO HAVE US CARTED OFF TO BAD-PERSON LIAR JAIL?!

"Oh we couldn't possibly ask you to do that," I stammered, as I began pulling all of her little one's (Ashley's?) daycare shit out of her cubby and shoving it into her backpack. My God—the number of water bottles, backup clothes, diapers, bedsheets, and fucking socks! These kids owned more property than I did. *Also, note to self,* I thought as I stood back from the now empty cubbies, *this thing will make quite a fine wine rack.*

"I don't mind at all," Katrina continued, flatly. "Really, you guys have worked so hard . . . it's the least I can do." Her monotone made it clear that she had our number. She *was* going to try to send us to Bad-Person Liar Jail.

And look, Katrina, if you're reading this: I get it. Finding a daycare in New York City is a fucking nightmare. With the tours and the deposits and the making sure it's a good fit for the kid and convenient-ish for you, it's such a hassle that it makes you wonder why you ever wanted to have kids in the first place. You committed to our daycare and thought that your horrible search was over, only to have to start again from scratch. After only a week. Under somewhat dodgy circumstances. Okay, we were in the wrong. But like, what was your endgame here? To catch us in a lie and then try to force us to stay open? Your daughter, whatever the hell her name is, ate half a box of waffles, spent two hours in a stroller, and then watched a four-year-old take a shit on the street. All in one day. Demand more for your child, Katrina. Reach higher. You can do better than this, Katrina. You can do better.

But no such explanation proved necessary to get Katrina off our case. Because there was a sudden BOOM from the apartment below us, and then the onset of the distinct, deep, bass sound of our neighbor's techno playlist. It's nightclub music, and in the right environment, I'm sure it's incredibly fun to listen to. But not after the longest week of my life, when the only thing standing between me and a gallon of freezer vodka was an angry, litigious parent. The music was so loud that the room shook around us. Daisy covered her ears.

"What the hell is that?" Katrina shouted. I could barely hear her.

"My neighbor," I said, nonchalantly. I hated that fucking guy, but I suddenly realized he was doing us a real solid right now. He was about to keep us out of Bad-Guy Liar Jail.

"Does this happen all day?" she shouted, incredulously.

I pretended not to hear her. "WHAT?" I screamed.

"DOES THIS HAPPEN ALL FUCKING DAY?" she shouted again.

I clutched my imaginary pearls, feigning shock that she had cursed during a "professional conversation," and in front of her fucking kid, what's-her-name.

"Sorry," she said. Again, just to enrage her, I lifted an eyebrow to imply that I hadn't heard her.

"I'M SORRRRRY!" she screamed again. She was at the end of her rope.

"THIS DOES HAPPEN PERIODICALLY!" I yelled. "IT'S WHY THEY DON'T NAP."

Katrina just shook her head in disbelief. She grabbed her kid, the bag of her kid's many belongings, and left. As soon as the door shut, I lunged at the freezer. I grabbed the vodka, considered shaking Steve and me a couple of martinis, but decided instead to cut to the chase: We needed shots, immediately. I poured two small glasses, handed one to Steve, and we threw them back. Sweet relief.

Unfortunately, the music from downstairs had gotten even louder and was now rattling the glasses in our cabinets. We'd been dealing with our downstairs neighbor and his music for years by that point, but it had gotten progressively worse. At first it was just random techno Fridays, maybe once a month or so. It was loud and annoying, but we dealt with it because it wasn't super frequent and because we . . . didn't have the greatest track record with neighbors.

We'd moved to this neighborhood from our apartment much farther uptown—the building where Fremme Drag Mom lived. An older man had lived above us there in a rent-controlled apartment that, according to the building's super, had been in the guy's family for generations. He was a smoker. And a bath taker. And himself an intolerably loud music listener. And like some kind of multitasker from hell, he liked to do all of these things at the same time. Nightly, it seemed, he would crank up his music, light up a carton of cigarettes, and splash around for hours in his bathtub. To make matters worse, the man was . . . quite large and the bathtubs in these rundown uptown apartments were quite small. So as he whooped it up in his toddler-sized tub, water would slosh over the sides, pouring through our bathroom ceiling while our walls shook and cigarette smoke seeped in.

We tolerated this for months, barely sleeping and watching the ceiling in our bathroom swell up like a balloon. And then one night, the ceiling literally popped and a mixture of brown sludge—which itself was probably a mixture of old-man sewage and filthy bathwater—cement, drywall, and metal pipes fell into our bathtub and all over the bathroom floor. Honestly, if Steve or I had been in the shower, we would have been killed—knocked unconscious and then drowned in a sea of loose stool. Nobody—well, hardly anybody—deserves to die that way.

After that near-miss sliming, we took to showering at the gym. And if we were home when our neighbor began running his bath, we'd start tapping on our ceiling with a broom handle, gently at first, to remind him that, having not been lethally doused by his filth, we were still living down here. We did this soft broomstick-tapping routine for a week and nothing changed, so one night I tapped louder: TAP! TAP! TAP! There was silence for a few seconds, then some sloshing, followed by a loud, pointed sequence: THUD! THUD! THUD!

I gasped and looked at Steve. *Was this guy seriously thudding my taps?* The music hadn't stopped, the smoking hadn't stopped, he'd just rolled himself out of the bath to fuck with us by THUDDING back at me.

"That motherfucker," I said as I threw the broom on the floor and turned toward the door.

"Patrick! DON'T!" Steve shouted. He wasn't specific about what I shouldn't do because he didn't need to be. I very rarely make the right decision, especially under stress. But fuck it; this guy had tortured us long enough.

I stormed out of our apartment and up the stairs to his door. The music was echoing throughout the whole building. How was I the only person upset about this?! I closed my fist and pounded on the door with all my strength. BANG! BANG! BANG! BANG!—I was not going to stop until he answered. Of course, *this* got the attention of all the neighbors, who opened their doors, scowling, wondering what the racket was. Could they not hear the music? Had they just learned to live with it? Did they fucking like it!? It didn't matter. If I had to kick the door in, the music was ending tonight. I was about to become their goddamn hero, setting them free from this filthy, loud despot.

Finally, I heard some movement from inside the apartment. I took a breath. No need to come in too hot. I would try to reason with the guy. I mean, we were neighbors, right? And everyone loves a nice bath. It was all a matter of moderation and respect, after all. Steve was about to be pretty impressed by me; I'd be reasonable, measured, and save the day.

The door unlocked and snapped open. A very angry, portly, middle-aged man with a cigarette dangling from his lips stood before me, clutching a butcher knife in his right hand.

"OH SHIT!" I heard one of the neighbors yell. "HE'S GOT A KNIFE AGAIN!"

AGAIN? I thought. *WHAT?*

Out of the corner of my eye, I saw a flash and ducked just in time to miss the knife slashing at my face.

"Run, kid!" a different neighbor shouted. "Pedro is crazy. He *will* stab you!"

"What on EARTH?" I screamed in . . . not my most masculine voice. I turned and ran down the hallway.

Pedro gave chase for only a second before stopping and waving the knife in my direction. "FUCK YOU, ASSHOLE!" he screamed. "NEXT TIME I'LL STAB YOU IN THE FUCKING EYE!"

"It's true, he will!" agreed another neighbor, from behind a partially closed door. "That man is nuts."

"YES I KNOOOOOOOW!" I screeched, as I fled back down the stairs.

Incidentally, this is why Steve gives me an open-ended "DON'T" whenever he sees me going to the crazy place. He understands that, metaphorically speaking, the world is full of insane, knife-wielding neighbors just looking for a reason to stab me in the eye. Steve is an old soul; he's wise and learns lessons quickly. I am the opposite. I stumble through the world making impulsive decisions resulting in avoidable mistakes. I'm a fool, prone to error. And I have advice for other fools out there: Find yourself an old soul to protect you from the neighbors who bathe. Who knows how many neighbors, bathers, and adjacent knife wielders I have avoided through Steve's wise DON'Ts.

We were in that apartment for another six months before we were able to move into the place that eventually became the daycare. We'd specifically asked if the neighbors were quiet, and we were assured that they were. And you know what? That was the truth. Until it wasn't. Like I said, the downstairs neighbor had gone from only occasionally blasting nightclub music to blasting it every Friday night, then every Friday *and* Saturday night, until it ultimately became an everyday occurrence. They'd start at 5 PM and go until two or three in the morning.

In short, it had gotten bad. And now, with the stress of the daycare closing, standing in the kitchen pouring us our second round of

SKYY vodka shots while the apartment shook around us, I was at a breaking point. "I can't take it," I said. "I'm going to lose my mind."

Steve didn't speak. He saw that I was going to the crazy place, but this time he wasn't going to stop me.

"I'm getting the basketball!" I said.

Steve nodded, his eyes narrowing. He was going to the crazy place with me. "Daisy!" he yelled. "BRING DADDY HIS TAP SHOES!"

The three of us met in the living room a minute later. Steve and I rolled up the rug. I lifted the basketball over my head and then threw it onto the floor as hard as I possibly could. And then I did it again. And again.

From on top of the coffee table, Steve shouted, "Five! Six! Seven! Eight!" and then leapt onto the floor, where he clomped and jumped and just plain stomped on the floor. Daisy squealed with confused delight as he scooped her up and yelled, "AND NOW LET'S SHUF-FLE OFF TO BUFFALO!" as I continued to pound the floor with the basketball.

Did any of this make one sliver of difference with our neighbors? Nope. Not one bit. We had truly, finally, completely lost our minds. And it felt fucking great.

. . . .

We slept in the next day. Our hangovers demanded it. When we finally got out of bed and dressed, we dragged ourselves and Daisy to the playground down the street. While she played, Steve and I worried. The daycare had been my life plan. And Steve had pivoted from finding a job after completing his second degree to making sure I didn't accidentally murder the children at our daycare. The daycare had been *it*. Now that it was closed, our little bit of income was gone.

Well, not totally gone. We did have one small income stream. She weighed about twenty-eight pounds and was currently going down the slide. Yes, because Daisy's adoption hadn't gone through and she was technically still in foster care, the State of New York was paying our family $618 per month.

"Our toddler is the breadwinner of our family," Steve said, glumly.

"Is that even allowed?" I asked. "Like, could we lose her if the state somehow finds out that we're income-less?" The question was too terrifying to answer. There was no time to lick our wounds; we needed jobs STAT.

Luckily, anyone who interviews Steve loves him. He's charming, brilliant, and can go with the flow. A major hospital hired my hot math nerd as a data manager within a few days.

As for me, I wanted a complete career change. Prior to the daycare, I'd spent the entirety of my post-college years working in hospitality—as a barista, bartender, waiter, and hotel concierge—each one of those a night job with an erratic schedule. Since I was starting my whole goddamn life over now, I wanted something more stable, like an engaging nine-to-five where I could learn a new set of skills *and* be home for dinner and bedtime. Perhaps the most ridiculous words I'll say in this book are the following: I developed a near obsession with the idea of becoming an executive assistant.

The ridiculousness of this idea has nothing to do with the job itself, but rather with the main requirements of this job: being organized, having a near-obsessive attention to detail, and a proficiency with something called "Microsoft Excel." It goes without saying that I have none of those things. But I was determined. And I gotta say: A determined me is essentially unstoppable—remember when I opened a daycare? Becoming an executive assistant, I hoped, would give me those adult character traits I'd never had: I'd learn to be calm, thoughtful, measured, and dare I say even quiet (sometimes)? The job would make me a real grown-up with a steady paycheck and, gasp, health insurance! I was *going* to be an executive assistant, God damn it. And I was going to be terrible at it. But with Goddess as my witness, I was gonna make it happen.

Even I understood that there was no way I was going to get hired in any sort of corporate setting. I needed something smaller and cooler where my personality and sass (read: gaaaaaay!) would be the unspoken qualification that would get me over the line. So it seemed like kismet when I found a posting on Craigslist—yes, *Craigslist*—for an executive assistant job at a major Broadway production house. Surely showfolk—my people, after all—would appreciate a dose of personality more than someone who knows how to use the Microsofts.

As I threw together a resume full of lies, Steve peered over my shoulder, imploring me to stop. "Why are you doing this? This is a *bad* idea."

It for sure was a bad idea, but I didn't care. Aren't you supposed to fake it till you make it or whatever? Plus, I had the last laugh because that resume full of lies actually got me an interview!

My interview was with Marianne from human resources. I'd later find out that she was the only employee of that department, which helped explain why she looked so exhausted and over it before my interview even began. She was middle-aged and tired. Her defenses were down; there was no way she would be able to withstand the assault of my personality. *Score!* I thought.

"Hi," she said, without extending her hand. She didn't ask my name; she just sat down and got to the relevant questions. "How are you with Excel?"

"Great!" I lied. *There was that word again*, I thought. *Is it "X.L."?* I made a mental note to look it up later, even though I knew I wouldn't.

"And PowerPoint?"

"Equally proficient," I said excitedly. That was the truth; I was equally unfamiliar with both. But "PowerPoint" sounded like fun!

"How about Google Calendar?"

"Ugh, I'm *obsessed*," I said, genuinely excited to have just learned that Google made calendars.

"And I'm assuming you're good with PivotTables?"

"Absolutely," I said, confidently. Food service was in my wheel-house; I'd set up tables, moved tables, pivoted tables—you name it.

"Fine. Is there anything else you think we should know about you?" she yawned, the boredom dripping from her mouth as she read the question word for word from the paper in front of her. Oh my God, I was losing her.

"I make a theater podcast!" I blurted out.

I expected her to say something snarky like "Congratulations" as she flipped her little binder closed and got up to leave. But instead, she perked up. "Really? Tell me about that," she said.

"Oh, um, okay," I said. I hadn't planned to talk about my pod-cast; I had planned to lie, be charming, find out what she wanted to hear, and just say that. I hadn't expected to share anything real about myself. "Well, I started listening to podcasts a few years ago when I was commuting to a hotel job. It was a long commute and I found a podcast where this guy interviewed big Broadway stars. It was amaz-ing. Well, actually, it was kind of dry—you know: question, answer, question, answer. But being a theater kid, I just loved it. It was great having that kind of access to people I'd always idolized. Anyway, the guy eventually stopped making the podcast, and I just assumed someone else would start making it. But nobody did. And I *needed* that podcast to exist. So I decided I was gonna make my own version of it."

"Wow," Marianne said. She was back. Which was great, but now buckle in, because this idiot is about to quote Toni Morrison.

I continued, "The writer Toni Morrison says 'if there's a book you want to read that hasn't been written yet, then you must write it.'" This got a raised eyebrow from Marianne. (Yes, it was a bit much, but I really wanted this fucking job.)

I went on to explain that learning how to make that podcast was the hardest thing I'd ever done—I didn't know anything about audio, recording, editing, or even how to convince guests to let me interview them. But I figured it out because I'm a hard worker.

What I didn't say—because I felt like I'd used up my allotted amount of drama with that Toni Morrison quote—was that for the last two years, making that podcast had been a refuge for me. And I realize, dear reader, that this is the first time I'm telling *you* about the podcast. But what, was I going to interrupt that perfectly *hilarious* daycare chapter to tell you about my fun side-hustle passion project? Absolutely not, the Choco-Shitter story is too good. Also, let's all try to keep in mind that this is my *first* book, and I'm still getting the hang of "linear storytelling" or whatever, so cut a gay a little slack.

I started the podcast on a whim just as Steve and I got serious about having a kid. At the time it seemed like an absurd idea to add *another* thing to my to-do list when I was already working full-time, researching all the ways we might become parents, and prepping for a baby to come into our lives. But I couldn't help it; I felt driven to do it. And when have I ever done anything at the right time? It should have been a ridiculous commitment on top of all my other messiness, but it was the opposite. It grounded me. Throughout all the craziness of navigating the foster care system, and then the ups and downs of parenting, the absolute insanity of prepping to open a daycare, operating it for a week and then shutting it down—every week I had the podcast to keep me grounded. I loved it. I was good at it. It felt like making podcasts was the thing I was meant to do. But first, I needed to be *an executive assistant.*

. . . .

Somehow, my bullshitting worked and I landed the job. I spent my days trying to watch YouTube videos about PowerPoint and Excel, but I couldn't get my brain to absorb any of the information because who fucking cares? I missed emails. I never learned how to send a meeting invite, and do not get me started on the goddamn master's degree you need in order to figure out how to transfer landline calls. Like, what the fuck is up with that? Oh and . . . *and* my desk was within earshot of the accounting department, which consisted of two men who spent their entire days trading 9/11 conspiracy theories and fuming that Hillary hadn't yet been locked up for her emails. I was . . . not thriving.

Steve had taken to coming in after hours to build my spreadsheets. I swear to God, that man's ability to, like, add a row, elongate a column, or *use the SUM FUNCTION*—whatever that is—is one of the sexiest things about him. It is pure sorcery. Did you know you can put numbers in those little blocks and make them add themselves up? Steve told me that. X.L. is *wild*. At first he tried to teach me, but we both knew I was a lost cause. It was faster for him to just do it himself; so a lot of days Steve worked a full day, ran to pick Daisy up from daycare, and then came to my office after hours to work his wizardry. Swoon.

On nights like this, we'd set Daisy up in Marianne's office with a stack of printer paper and the shredder. She was obsessed. She would giggle and jump up and down, making munching sounds as the machine ate the paper. It was adorable. And a little bit scary, and oh my God are we the worst parents in the world?

One night I left her alone in Marianne's office longer than I should have. When I went in to check on her, I found that she had finished shredding the stack of printer paper and, with no adult around to tell her no, had moved on to the contents of a stack of manila folders sitting on Marianne's desk. Those folders contained all of the recently negotiated and signed contracts for a new off-Broadway musical the production company was mounting, a project the entire office had been working on for weeks. My unattended child had just fed almost all of the documents to her friend the shredder. "NUM NUM NUM!" she squealed, in delight. I was fired the next day.

· ·

I was now in a panic. This was two pretty big failures in a row. Not only was I jobless again, but this time I really had no idea how I was going to make money. Go back to restaurants? Hotels? Just the thought of having to pretend to like strangers for a living again . . . I was not going to make it.

This was when Steve gave me what I would come to refer to as "the magic talking-to." He thrust a cocktail into my hand and said, "It's time for you to go for it with podcasting. It's the only work that makes you happy. You have to just do it."

It was true. The longer I'd been making *Theater People*, the better I'd been getting at it. I was starting to feel like maybe I could find an opening in the world of podcasting and actually make enough money for it to be a real, legitimate job. Those of us paying attention to the industry were starting to see independent creators become successful enough to make their shows their full-time jobs. Why NOT me? For a while now, I'd been making jokes about emptying out our single closet and turning it into a podcast studio. Was Steve now suggesting that I actually do it?

"Can we afford it?" I asked.

"I think we can, for a little while at least," he said. "You have to try. It's the only thing you want to do. And anyway, you can't end up at another job where I'm making your spreadsheets, because then I'd have to kill you."

We both laughed.

"Okay. It's decided. You're a podcaster now," he said. And with those words, he set me free.

. . . .

This brings me to my partner in true crime: Gillian Pensavalle.

The first time I met Gillian in real life was at an unremarkable Starbucks on 48th Street in Midtown. I'd reached out to her a few weeks before because, like me, she made a theater podcast—hers was *The Hamilcast*, all about the Broadway musical *Hamilton*—and I thought we should know each other. I arrived at the Starbucks a little early and waited outside. I saw her a few minutes later, speed walking in what I would come to recognize as her signature outfit: black everything—boots, jeans, shirt, jacket. She was rushing and seemed a little flustered, and she beat me to the door handle. She absolutely did not recognize me as the person she was there to meet, but she smiled and did a little jig to move herself out of my way to hold the door open for *me* to go in *ahead* of her. Maybe it was just the unexpected—and adorably executed—kind gesture from a fellow New Yorker in the middle of the afternoon; maybe, and more likely, that mundane moment still resonates because I can trace all of the incredible ways my life changed for the better back to that moment. But for some reason, I've never forgotten that. That opened door was the gateway to a new life.

I didn't know that then, though, so all I said was, "Gillian?"

"Oh! Patrick! Hi!" she laughed as she leaned in for a hug.

"If you want to find some seats, I'll grab us coffees," I said. "How do you take yours?"

"Light. And. Sweet."

I gay-gasped. Those exact words, in that exact order, perfectly punctuated in that exact cadence could mean only one thing: "Oh my God! You're a Dunkin' Donuts girl just like me."

"All day, every day," she tossed back with a campy wink. I knew right then that this was the beginning of a beautiful friendship.

Over the weeks that followed, we saw each other a lot. Coffee dates turned into happy hour dates where we got to know each other. I quickly learned that Gillian is a great listener. Mention a handful of times that you love *The Golden Girls,* and for your next birthday, you'll get a framed architectural rendering of the home the women lived in—complete with an explanation from the architect himself about how the home as depicted in the show is an engineering impossibility. Drone on one night over endless bourbons on the rocks about an obscure gay civil rights hero named Craig Rodwell who you are obsessed with, but who has been lost to history, and for Christmas you'll get a framed old-timey photo of the guy that you never knew existed because Gillian dug through some historical archive to find it.

Gillian really hears you when you talk. And this, I think, is how we wound up working together. Because for weeks, whenever I saw her, I'd go on and on about how I felt a clock ticking—that Steve's "follow your dreams" speech had been sweet and empowering, but certainly it had an expiration date, right?

And then one afternoon, as we sidled up to the bar of our favorite midtown happy hour spot, both ordering white wine—me, correctly, a buttery Chardonnay; her, much less correctly, Pinot Grigio—both judging the other for ordering the wrong white wine, I said, "I've always been obsessed with true crime podcasts. And it seems like true crime is where independent creators can actually break through."

Sipping her wrong wine, she said the right thing: "Well, you know I'm obsessed with true crime too. Maybe we should do something together."

"YES!" I shrieked, startling both of us. I'd been thinking the same thing but had been too nervous to mention it. Gillian, I'd come to learn, is brilliantly funny, and quick, and smart. And there was something about the way our brains worked together . . . we didn't finish each other's sentences—we *continued* each other's sentences. We could talk for hours because we were constantly Yes And-ing like A+ improv students. And as a person who listens to podcasts as incessantly as Derek and his friends (hey, boo!) watch Marvel movies, I knew that that kind of banter was both rare and total podcast magic. If we did it right, we definitely had a hit show in us.

"Why don't we solve the Zodiac," she said, sort of casually.

"That is a *great* idea," I replied, glad that we'd settled on a plan. "Oh"—I had to pause—"but wait; if we want to make something we can monetize, it needs to be a weekly show. With Zodiac, we'd probably solve that in like seven or eight episodes."

Gillian nodded. "Oh, you're right. Okay, let's think of something else."

To be clear: the only reason we didn't make a podcast *solving the Zodiac case*—a case that detectives, investigative journalists with actual credentials, and the FB-*fucking*-I have spent decades trying and failing to solve—is because we wanted to make a weekly show. Sorry history: maybe we'll get around to it eventually before he kills again.

Given how entertaining *True Crime Obsessed* is, it will probably shock you to learn that originally I had no intention of making a *fun* podcast. Yes, I knew that Gillian and I were funny-ish and that we were starting to speak our own weird twin language—both fantastic ingredients for a popular podcast. But it was my full intention to harness our powers to make a true crime podcast for the nerds—we'd use big words! Reference classical music somehow! Be smart and witty enough to get us booked on *Fresh Air* with Terry Gross!!

And so, the idea I eventually pitched to Gillian was a podcast with three segments: a true crime news segment, an interview segment, and a middle segment where we'd recap a piece of true crime content. Because the news and interview segments required, like, research and writing, we sort of half-assed those parts, because, like, boring. But we threw ourselves wholeheartedly into prepping for the recap segment because it meant drinking wine and watching TV!

The Imposter was the first documentary we picked to recap, and to this day it remains one of the best true crime documentaries I've ever seen. It tells the story of the disappearance of a thirteen-year-old American boy, Nicholas Barclay, and the *full-grown, foreign-language-speaking man* who showed up IN SPAIN a mere three years later pretending to be him. Somehow, the boy's family bought the whole thing hook, line, and sinker. You truly can't make this stuff up.

On recording day, Gillian and I, having watched the documentary and taken notes separately, met up in my living room, plopped ourselves in front of a couple of microphones—podcasting is not a fancy art form, people—and just talked through the documentary and our reactions to it. Right from the start, it was exactly what we hoped it would be: like taking one of our happy hour conversations, with all of their big laughs and Yes Ands, and applying it to the ridiculousness of this true crime story.

The second we turned off the recorder, we knew that that was it—that was the podcast. We stared at each other sort of stunned for a second.

"That . . . was amazing," I said.

"Shit. Yeah, that was *AMAZING*," Gillian said back.

I could see what the podcast was meant to be so clearly now. We'd scrap the interview and news segments and just tell true crime stories by recapping documentaries based on different cases. It would be thoughtful, and rageful, and even funny since we both relied on humor to convey the anger we felt when talking about these crimes.

"So we're doing this?" I asked hopefully.

Gillian thought for a second. "Do you think the true crime world is ready for a flamboyant, screechy, gay guy, and a loud, opinionated woman?"

And then before I could answer, she said, "Fuck 'em. We're doing it anyway."

Chapter Ten

THE KITCHEN FLOOR SOCIAL CLUB

hree years into making *True Crime Obsessed*, my life felt stable. I was making real money for the first time, and I had managed to find a way to become my own boss while doing something that I absolutely loved. So screw you, daycare gods. Finally, things felt calm and steady. But isn't it always the way that just when we hit a smooth patch in life, some new drama appears, demanding our full attention? Or . . . does that just happen to me, the guy literally voted "most dramatic" by both his high school and college graduating classes. Don't I sound fun? Anyway, this new drama concerned my mother, who, you'll remember, is a lesbian.

I have always been obsessed with lesbians (probably because of my lesbian mother). A lot of it is the music—and do not come for me on this. It is scientifically proven that the Indigo Girls were created by Goddess at the intersection of Perfection and Iconic. It's also the clothes. And yes, I *know* not all lesbians prioritize the comfortable over the fashionable, but as a person who owns two pairs of jeans and six hundred black T-shirts—primarily my own cheap merch—the comfy lesbians are my people. But mostly I'm obsessed with lesbians because they are just quality fucking humans. You have never seen a group of people take care of those they love the way lesbians do. If you don't have a lesbian in your life, go out today and get one. You will thank me.

I know all this about lesbians because I've been surrounded by them for most of my life. My mom came out to my siblings and me when we were kids, right after she left my dad. In my memory, it was apropos of nothing and very matter-of-fact. We were all standing in the small hallway of our new little home, each of us in the doorway of our bedrooms.

"I'm going to be dating," my mother announced. "And I'm going to be dating women. Exclusively. Because I love women and I always have."

Was this the best she could have done? Probably not. But coming out is so SO incredibly awkward. Most of us summon the courage over months, pick a moment, and then blurt out whatever gets it done the fastest. When I, a decade later, came out over Thanksgiving dinner, I waited for a quiet moment and then shouted, "I'M GAY PASS THE POTATOES." My sisters make fun of me for this to this day. Mostly because, like, no announcement was ever going to be necessary, but also because for someone who likes every moment to be all about me, I clearly wanted that "big revelation" to pass quickly.

Anyway, from the moment my mother came out, she was forevermore surrounded by a squad of women who had her back through it all—poverty, getting sober, breakups, deaths, and the tragic and too-soon end of Lilith Fair. For my mom, it's been a lifetime of camaraderie that has proven especially vital in recent years.

My mom is in her early seventies, and for ten years she'd lived alone in a cute little apartment complex in the town of Brewster, Massachusetts. She moved there right after her wife, Carol, died. Carol, a bus driver (because stereotypes are sometimes based on real things, people!), had complained to my mom one afternoon that she was having trouble breathing. My mom brought her to the hospital where doctors found a grapefruit-sized tumor on one of her lungs. She died within the week. And despite the flurry of lesbians jumping in to support my mom any way they could (The cooking! The cleaning! The acoustic guitar circles and amateur woodworking!), my mom was obviously devastated.

Though she was sad to downsize to her little apartment after Carol's passing, it was a financial necessity. But my mom is eminently adaptable and, as she had all her life, she made new friends in her new building very quickly. Over the years, she became especially close to an elderly lesbian named Sue, who lived across the hall. Interestingly, my mother has a unique ability to always find the other lesbian in any given situation. Like at our middle school for example, where after a year of my winter concerts and my sister's track meets, my mother was suddenly hanging out socially with both the band teacher, Ms. L, and track coach, Ms. C, who my mom had determined were a couple. And she was right. My mom can spot a fellow lesbian from a mile away.

Anyway, one day in January of 2020, I called my mom. She always had so many friends in and out of her apartment that you never knew who would answer the phone. Though, of course, some options were better than others. For example, elderly-across-the-hall-lesbian, Sue, had had a stroke a few years back, and though fully functional in every other way, Sue was only able to say, at most, one word from each sentence she was trying to communicate. And I'm guessing that pre-stroke Sue was something of a chatterbox, because she had a *lot* to convey. For most people, talking to Sue in person required an exhausting amount of hand gestures and guessing. But not for my mom. Perhaps through some kind of Super Lesbian Emotional Telepathy, she always knew exactly what Sue was trying to say. Or maybe Sue just went along with her guesses because, as my mother loved to say, "She just wants to get into my pants." And to be fair, seemingly all of the lesbian octogenarian set on Cape Cod—a surprisingly abundant community—wanted a piece of my mom. My mom could get it.

But when I called this time, another one of Mom's friends answered: "Hi Patrick, it's Allison."

Oh thank goodness, I thought. I loved Sue, but I was never up for the twenty minutes of phone charades it took to get through the pleasantries. Allison was much easier to deal with. She and my mom had been close friends for over twenty years. Allison, I guess I should say, is not a lesbian. Which is too bad; she and my mom would have made a great couple. Still, they do spend enough time together that it's sort of like they *are* a couple, just without the sex. Which would never be enough for my mom. She loves the sex.

"Hi!" I said. "Is my mom home?" Dumb question, I guess. Of course my mother was home. For the previous year she'd been more or less confined to a wheelchair after a decades-long slide into immobility. There was no inciting event really; she had never been particularly active, and then over the years, she sort of just stopped moving altogether. Then her legs got weak, so when she did walk, she started falling, so the wheelchair became the safest option. "Yup, she's here. Hang on a second, she's on the floor in the kitchen."

"Oh man. She couldn't make it to the living room floor?"

"Nope, this one came on pretty fast. But don't worry—she's got that cat pillow she likes and a cup of tea."

From the kitchen floor, my mother yelled: "I'M PERFECTLY COMFORTABLE, PATRICK! DON'T WORRY ABOUT ME!"

Now if the casualness of this conversation between Allison and me sounds insane to you, it's because it is. You see, even the wheelchair wasn't enough for my mom anymore. And the truth is, it hadn't been enough for her for a while. For months, despite the seat belt and the footrest, every day she was slipping out of her wheelchair, and, because she didn't have the leg strength to stand or the upper-body strength to pull herself back up, she would just be on the floor indefinitely. In the beginning, this had been shocking. But somehow, someway, over time, she, I, her friends—we all came to accept this as a normal part of her day.

Does this make Allison, Sue, and me monsters? Maybe. But something to know about my mother is that she has always had an excessively good attitude about everything. Literally nothing bothers her. So the first time she slipped out of the chair—presumably fifteen minutes or so after she got into it for her inaugural sit—and found herself on the floor in the living room near her bookcase, she simply reached for a book, rolled herself over, and read. On the floor. For six (!) hours.

When she started to get hungry and realized that she was going to have to use the bathroom sooner or later, she just calmly yelled for across-the-hall Sue. Horny Sue, who truly did look for any excuse to visit my mother, was there in seconds. Obviously, Sue couldn't lift my mother back into her chair, so they called Allison. Allison gave it a go, but also couldn't manage it. And so, after mulling it over, they called the non-emergency number of the local police precinct and explained the situation. The cops sent EMTs who were able to hoist her back into the chair.

This situation was rinsed and repeated so many times that my mother's episodes on the floor became more of a social occasion than anything else. Like bizarro party planners, my mom and her friends prepared for the next inevitable slip. Sue stocked my mom's cabinets with spill-proof travel mugs that my mom could drink out of at any angle. And Allison went on library runs and brought board games galore. The three of them would gather wherever my mom had slipped and just spend entire days together playing games, reading books, and eating meals on the floor. Of course, they hoped that the fall would take place on the living room carpet instead of the cold kitchen floor, but the party went on regardless of venue.

Ultimately, this informal Kitchen Floor Social Club would decide to pack it in for the day and call EMS to come put my mom back in her chair. The reason they would wait so long to call for help was because they didn't want me to know just how often this was happening, and they knew that Jarrod would rat them out to me. Jarrod, by the way, was the first responder who . . . first responded the first time my mom was on the floor. He was very sweet and kind, and he grew to really care about my mom, so over the weeks, he sort of made it his business to be the one to answer the calls to my mom's place. But he was getting more and more concerned. Eventually, he asked my mom for my phone number and called me.

"I'm happy to help your mom whenever she needs, but you know she can't go on living like this much longer, right?" he said in a *very* sexy Boston-adjacent accent.

"I know," I said, wondering if I could finagle a last name out of him so I could pop over to Instagram and see if he was one of those EMT bros who post shirtless gym selfies.

"There are plenty of nice nursing homes on the Cape that would take great care of your mom *and* wouldn't cost you a penny because they're fully funded by Medicaid."

But that—the move to the nursing home itself, not the cost—was the thing. That was why this particular failure of mine—a failure to make sure my mom was living out her golden lesbian years in relative safety—had gone on as long as it had. Because the next and final step in her life was Shady fucking Pines. (Which is a *Golden Girls* nursing home reference. Hi, Derek! You still with us?)

On *The Golden Girls,* Shady Pines was the nursing home that Sophia vowed to never return to: "I'm telling you, Dorothy—they used to pre-sell our bodies to medical schools." And of course, I knew that *The Golden Girls* wasn't reality—after all, you're telling me four fabulous women go seven seasons in *Miami* without *one* drunken night at a gay bar? I think not—but still, the image stuck. And I think knowing that the nursing home was next was also why Sue and Allison were willing to spend entire days playing Monopoly on the floor with my mom. They were the last safeguard against her moving into a home, which also maybe wasn't all that far away for them too. We were in a bit of denial.

• •

It was hard to see my mom's body finally bottoming out. For those of us who love her, there has always been a sort of frustrated hopefulness that if she would *just get up and take a walk,* maybe she would get that active spark back. Then, maybe she could come to New York City to see what I've done with my life and spend some real quality time with Daisy. Or drive up to Boston and spend the afternoon with my sister Sarah and her two boys. Or, gasp, get on an airplane and go see my other sister's kid—the grandchild she's only met once! Instead, we were now facing the reality: a wheelchair or a bed or a couch would very likely be the only places any of us would spend time with her again.

Of course, it hadn't always been like this. My mom had been young and virile once. In fact, one of her favorite time periods to tell us about is the year after her high school graduation when she was an eighteen-year-old basketball coach—you really can't make this stuff up—at a stuffy Connecticut boarding school. And if this sounds like it's about to get super lesbian, reader, it is. You see, according to my mother, this was the year of her big lesbian sexual awakening, which may or may not have been sparked by the fact that during this time, her star player was none other than a seventeen-year-old Glenn Close. Yes, THAT Glenn Close. Mom always told us that she and Glenn had been . . . well, *close*—especially the summer *after* Glenn graduated, when she became a full legal adult and my mother was no longer in, like, a position of authority in her life. (You really *can't* put too fine a point on these things.) Anyway, since this was my mother's first big lesbian summer, I always wondered if there had been more between her and Glenn. I asked my mom about this a lot because I am insufferable. And she always refused to answer in any definitive way, which allowed me to assume—and tell everyone I ever met—that yes, my mom had in fact gone to lesbian pound town with the woman who would go on to be *ROBBED* of an Oscar Eight! Freaking! Times! Honestly, what is wrong with us?

But really, it was an open question. And this question—"*Did my mom sleep with Glenn Close?*"—became a family mystery I vowed to solve. I always swore that if I ever met Glenn Close in the wild, I would just come right out and ask her.

Then, in the winter of 2014, it seemed like I might get my one and only chance. Steve and I had a friend who had just shot a television series with Glenn. This friend, who, at their request, shall remain nameless, comes from a legacy Hollywood family that always throws an epic Christmas party full of famous people. It's always the highlight of my year. Because of the famous people.

Knowing there was a good chance Glenn might be there, Steve and I came up with a plan—by which I mean that I came up with a plan that Steve, for days, tried to talk me out of. "Can you please not ask Glenn Close if she fucked your mom," Steve begged, trying to reason with me.

"Babe, how could I *NOT*? This is probably the only shot I'll ever have."

"It's none of your business!" he shouted.

Excuse me, but if solving a family mystery is none of my business, then what exactly *is* my business?

Daisy was just nine months old at the time. Normally we'd get a sitter for the night because the real famous people never even got to this party before midnight, and if you're not doing 2 AM shots with Sarah Paulson, did the party even happen? But there would be no babysitter this year because Daisy was part of my ingenious plan. Daisy *WAS* the plan. I was going to put her in the baby harness over my stomach, face her out, and just aim her at any famous person I wanted to chat with. With her chubby little cherub face, deep-brown eyes, and long, thick, black hair, she would be irresistible bait, luring in any A-lister we wanted to interro—er, talk to.

The party was at a loft in SoHo that had been in our friend's family for decades. It was massive but still somehow always felt warm and homey, especially around the holidays. Walking in, we saw Paul Giamatti alone in a corner, drinking a beer, like every year.

"Jesus, that guy," Steve said.

"I know," I said. "I've never seen him talk to *anybody* at one of these things." I was careful not to aim Daisy at him and waste our precious party time. We checked our coats and walked into the living room. John Lithgow was sitting on the couch sipping a glass of wine.

"That's the fucking *Harry and the Hendersons* guy!" I scream-whispered at Steve. "I want to meet him."

"Me too," Steve said. So I walked a little farther into the room and pointed Daisy right at him. And then bam:

"A BABY!" Lithgow shouted in his signature half yodel. "Bring that baby over here," he said, as he jumped off the couch and made room for me. *Wow*, I thought, patting Daisy on the head, *that worked even better than expected.*

As he cooed over Daisy, suddenly, a hush came over the party and the crowd parted as a woman in a long winter coat—carrying an enormous Casio keyboard, of all things—made her way toward us.

"Ah, Glenn is here," Lithgow said. He started walking away, excusing himself: "I should go give her a hand. She's gonna be leading the Christmas carol sing-along."

Steve and I both gay-gasped and pearl clutched. What in Homosexual Christmas Heaven was Lithgow talking about? But now was not the time for follow-up questions.

Looking annoyed, Glenn was giving off strong *do not speak to me unless I speak to you* vibes, so everyone stayed huddled in their little groups all just, like, staring at her.

But I wouldn't be intimidated. I stuck to the plan and moved to the center of the room. Then I positioned an eye-rolling Steve so that we could talk in a way that looked natural, while still pointing Daisy, unobstructed, straight at Close. Close, meanwhile, still holding the five-foot-long keyboard, was now in an animated conversation with Anjelica Huston and Lithgow. *Jesus, what on earth were the three of them talking about? Please let it be a* Harry and the Hendersons *sequel . . .*

Then, all of a sudden, Daisy started to cry. *Fuck! No! Noooo!* I thought. *You're supposed to be cute! And cuddly! Make the Famouses want to hold you!*

Glenn looked over at us. Was she annoyed? I quickly unsnapped Daisy, spun her around to put her head on my shoulder, and started bouncing—the only motion that ever worked to get her to stop crying. But it was not helping this time, and the crying was just getting worse. I turned around to look at Steve. His eyes grew wide.

"What?" I said. He nodded his head, indicating something behind me. I turned back around just in time to see Glenn quickly approaching. Holy shit. It was Icon O'Clock and I. Was. Not. Ready.

The look on Close's face was all business. She did not seem like she was in the mood to share her sapphic memories with me, even if I could get Daisy to stop crying. But I had to ask, so I opened my mouth—and then it happened so fast: like a fucking traffic cop, she put one hand in my face in the "stop" position, indicating that I had not been given permission to speak. With the other hand, she did the "gimme that" fingers, gesturing toward my screaming kid. I looked at Steve, who gave me nothing. I looked back at Close, who, tired of waiting, just snatched Daisy from my arms. She then turned, and, *with my child,* walked back to Lithgow and Huston.

And then Steve and I . . . just stood there. Staring.

"Did Glenn Close just kidnap our fucking kid?" I asked, stunned.

"Yup," Steve said.

"Do we go over there?"

"I . . . don't think so," Steve said, as we watched Glenn shoo Gia-matti away and then turn her back on him as she rejoined the icons. Cruella De Vil was in no mood.

Steve was mad, but I wasn't about to acknowledge it. I mean, I love my husband, and I guess I get why he'd "be concerned" about a "total stranger" up and "walking off with our kid" but, like, this whole situa-tion was *so* bizarre and I was loving every second of it. I mean, here we were in this room full of incredibly famous people (surrounded by food but nobody eating a morsel, I might add), and the most famous of them all was now babysitting our kid for free? Stories like this are currency among the gays. I'd get mileage out of this one at brunches and happy hours and Tony Award parties for years to come. AND AND AND (!) there was no way this situation didn't end with a face-to-face with Close. I mean, she had to return Daisy at some point, right? Grumpy husband be damned, it was all upside as far as I was concerned.

And then, bam: Glenn Close began quietly making her way back to us, with a sleeping Daisy in her arms.

"Do not ask her if she fucked your mother. Do *not* ask her if she fucked your mother," Steve hissed through gritted teeth.

"Sorry, babe," I hissed back, trying not to move my lips, "this is happening."

When she reached us, Glenn said, "Well, she gave me a run for my money, but my guess is she's down for the night now."

Oh God, this was my chance. If I was ever going to find out if she got a piece of my mom, it was going to be now. "Thanks so much," I said, gently taking my baby back. And then: "Hey, can I ask you a question?" I felt Steve dig his nails into my shoulder.

"Sure," Glenn said. She was 100 percent not in the mood for a question.

Steve jumped in before I had a chance to speak, hoping to avert disaster: "His mom says she knows you from your private school days."

"Hmm, what was her name?" Glenn asked.

"Pamela Parker," I said. Glenn seemed to consider this, like she was going through some kind of Rolodex in her head. "She was your basketball coach, and then you two became close friends after you graduated?"

Reader, I swear to you, Glenn Close's eyes widened with some kind of memory, and she let out the tiniest chuckle. Steve's grip on my shoulder transitioned from a clawed warning to an OMG squeeze.

"Well," Glenn said with a smile. "If she says she was there, then she must have been." And then, wait! Was that a wink? *Did Glenn Close just wink at us*?? "Now, please excuse me. I have to go set up for the caroling."

As she walked away, Steve whispered into my ear, "Oh my God. Glenn Close totally banged your mom." Case, um, Close-d.

. . . .

A few years after her Close Encounter of the Maybe Lesbian Kind, my mom met my dad and the two got married. The details surrounding this choice, for both of them, have always been a bit murky to me. As best I can tell, for my mom, it came down to wanting kids. She preferred women, and says she made that clear to my father. But this was the seventies, decades before the gays were pairing off and raising families and curating insufferable Instagram accounts full of perfect intergenerational Halloween costumes that the rest of us could never possibly live up to. Yes, I am talking to you, Neil Patrick Harris.

As for why my father married my mother—and this is going to sound really romantic, so, you know, dim the lights and turn up the Yanni—I've always assumed he did it because he thought she might be the only woman willing to marry *him*. He was born with a mild-ish form of cerebral palsy that left him with a lifelong, constant, and very obvious full-body tremor. It didn't affect him much physically, but, of course, because everyone is the worst, people tormented him for it. So when he met my mom and she eventually seemed open to the possibility of marriage, he didn't care what her reasons were; he went for it. Essentially, it was a marriage of convenience for both of them.

And if this sounds to you like the makings of a cold, passionless, miserable marriage and cohabitation, reader, you are nailing it! They divorced fourteen years later, just before my mother's fortieth birthday. My mom had tried conforming to bland heteronormativity, but it didn't take. Who knows, maybe if my dad hadn't been a chain-smoking, unevolved, emotionally unavailable misogynist with little to no interest in raising children, it could have worked.

And let me tell you, when my mother made the decision to take the kids and leave, she did it with such dramatic—and probably unnecessary—flair, it's as though I planned the escape myself.

She and my older sister Sarah woke me and my younger siblings up in the middle of the night holding flashlights and *pillowcases* full of clothes. Again, I love the commitment to the bit, but I can say with full confidence now, this was a little over the top, ladies. Like, regular suitcases would have been fine. They told us we needed to be quiet as we tiptoed down the stairs and out the front door. We all piled into my mom's car, and then, really leaning into *The Sound of Music* of it all, my mom put it in neutral and *pushed it* out of the driveway and down the block while twelve-year-old Sarah sat at the wheel and steered. It wasn't until we rounded the corner that my mom climbed in, turned the car on, shoved a Melissa Etheridge tape into the deck, because of course, and drove us off into the night.

Truth be told, we weren't in any real danger. My dad was a grump and he'd made the living situation untenable, but he wasn't violent. I honestly don't think he would have put up much of a fight about us leaving. My mom just wasn't taking any chances; she was ready to get on with her life and had decided to leave, so the cleanest break was to disappear in the middle of the night. And to do it with a little bit of flair.

We soon resettled on Cape Cod, where my mom struggled to support herself and her four kids. Unbeknownst to me, she was also struggling with her alcoholism. While I do remember a time early on in our new life on Cape Cod where my mom kept a bottle of Jim Beam on the kitchen counter next to the toaster, I do not have a single memory of seeing my mother drink out of it or of her ever being drunk. I'm not saying my mother wasn't an alcoholic; I *am* saying that I don't have any stories about being forgotten at the grocery store or waking up to a present-less Christmas morning with her passed out in a Santa suit. These would have come in really handy in a comedy memoir, though, Mom, so thanks for nothing on that front.

She joined Alcoholics Anonymous soon after we settled on the Cape, and this is where Pamela got her groove back. She took the program very seriously. Or, I should say, she took *most* of the program very seriously. She went to meetings on the daily, got a sponsor, and banished the Jim Beam; but the one tenet my mom was a little more loosey-goosey with was the one prohibiting dating until reaching a full year of sobriety. The rule is sensible because apparently relationships are one of the leading causes of relapse, but my mom took a hard pass on that directive.

Truly, one of my favorite things about my mother during this time was just how completely slutty she was. And I mean that from the heart. Not to turn this *hilarious* book into some kind of boring dissertation, but the LGBTQ community has a long history of, let's call it liberal sexual expression after periods of sexual repression. Straight women, remember when you got to college and met your first gay, probably named Xander? You thought you'd died and gone to best friend heaven. But then you found that you didn't get to hang out much because Xander was always on Grindr looking for sex? And you were annoyed and maybe a little hurt?

It's not that he didn't love you right back, it's that just that after a lifetime of being bullied and/or having nothing but his own hand for a sexual outlet, sweet Xander was now experiencing the vast ocean of dick available to him for the very first time. And he was diving in.

So after fourteen years of, I'm sure, sexually repressed marriage to my dad, this forty-year-old lesbian was single and ready to mingle. And let me tell you, Cape Cod lesbian AA was more than happy to provide, bringing a troupe of very interesting women into our lives, even if ever so briefly:

- First, there was Danielle the Truck Driver. She was an energetic woman in her early thirties who loved to cook for us and also *loved* having sex with our mom. There was a lot of "closed door time" when Danielle was around.
- Next were Kate and Kate. One was a gym teacher, the other an accountant. They were both stern but friendly, and my siblings and I didn't interact with them very much. It wasn't until I was in college that I looked back and realized that

my mom had been in a Kate-Mom-Kate throuple for a little while. Get it, Mom!

- Then there was Diane the Mail Carrier. Diane was hot. She was a little older than my mom, but super fit. She was built like a professional tennis player with a sick body and short black hair. I was fascinated by her. Toward the end of her brief affair with my mom, she told me she'd be gone for the summer; she was off to the Greek isle of Lesbos, "the birthplace of Sappho and lesbianism," she said. I was twelve. I had no idea what she was talking about, but man did she sound excited. We never did see Diane again.

- And of course, there was Heidi Heartlock, which is hands down the greatest lesbian last name of all time. Heidi Heartlock left a mark on my mother. Like, to this day, whenever my mother talks about her, she always uses her full name, like how regular people talk about celebrities. Heidi Heartlock was bookish and nerdy and, unfortunately, married. To a man. I don't know how she and my mom met or how long their affair lasted, the only thing I know for sure about Heidi Heartlock is that she was apparently a beast in the sack. My mother told me this once when I unabashedly asked her who her best lay was. (I mean, I'd lived with her through her super slutty years. I had a right to know.)

"Heidi Heartlock" she said before I could even finish the question. "No doubt. Heidi Heartlock was the best sex I ever had." She took a pause. "It was more than sex, Patrick. It was passionate lovemaking." Which . . . is what I get, I guess, for asking the question. Poor, stunned, red-faced Steve was just collateral damage.

· ·

The point to all of this is just to say that my mother had lived a very full and mostly happy life. Very lesbionic. She'd (Maybe?? Probably??) bedded Glenn Close, been married to a man, had four kids, made passionate love to a Heidi Heartlock many, many, many times, and she'd even had a dog named Serenity—I mean, that's basically a whole Indigo Girls album right there.

So when I called that night and found out that she had slipped out of her wheelchair and had spent hours on the kitchen floor *again*, I knew it was finally time to take probably-hot EMT Jarrod's advice and do something about it. This was a failure I needed to fix. A nursing home wasn't death; it was just the next phase. And knowing my mother, she'd be boning one of the nurses in no time.

When we finally talked about it, nobody put up much of an argument. My mom, Sue, and Allison all knew that the situation wasn't sustainable. With Hot Jarrod's help, we were able to find a nursing home in my mom's town with open visiting hours so Sue and Allison could visit her at any time. Soon the Kitchen Floor Social Club would reconvene, this time hopefully on chairs.

And I gotta say, my mom, God bless her, made this so easy for me. Once it was decided, she started complaining about how her apartment was too big, and a bit drafty, and there was never anyone around, and how she couldn't wait to be in a place where there would be doctors and nurses available all the time and where she'd have a roommate to chat with. Sure, some people's moms would just be saying that to make their son feel better. *My* mom was not. She was genuinely excited. Yes, the food would suck, but within a week she'd have a hundred new friends. She wanted me to know she'd be okay.

After moving her into the home, my older sister Sarah and I cleared out the apartment she'd lived in for the last ten years, sifting through keepsakes from her incredible life. In one of my mom's photo albums, I found a picture of her sitting in a chair in the middle of a party, surrounded by her community of friends. All of my siblings are there too, and we're all almost grown up. Everyone is smiling, especially my mom. I'm standing behind her with an electric razor, about to shave her head. She'd been diagnosed with breast cancer a few months prior and was about to start chemotherapy. I'd almost forgotten about this day: her "Lose Your Hair on Your Own Terms" Party. *Wow*, I thought. *This was such a powerful—*

"OH MY GOD! OH MY FUCKING GOD!" Sarah screamed from the bedroom, interrupting my moment. She ran into the living room, clutching a pillowcase. Closing her eyes, she turned it upside down, spilling the contents on the rug. Out fell three enormous dildos. One tan, one pink, and one jet-black.

This was for sure more traumatizing for Sarah than it was for me. Sarah had always had trouble accepting our mother as a sexual being. I, on the other hand, always knew that our mom was a little bit of a freak.

"I can do you one better," I said to her.

"Impossible," she said, shaking her head. "Please don't."

But I couldn't help myself. I love making Sarah cringe. I walked over to the bookshelf and pulled out one of my mother's "God Journals." These were journals where she talked directly to God and/or Jesus. Now look, normally I wouldn't approve of reading other people's private shit. But I'd found this particular journal open on my mother's desk the day after we moved her to the nursing home. I swear I read it by ACCIDENT. And anyway, my mom has since given me permission to share.

"Okay," I said to my sister, thumbing to the page. "This is dated October 2, 1996."

"Oh God," Sarah said.

"Literally," I responded.

"What?"

"*Many nights I've imagined You inside me, oh Lord . . .* " I read.

"WHAT THE FUCK IS THAT?" Sarah screamed.

" *. . . What would it be like to experience Your manhood, oh Lord?*"

"OH MY GOD—IT'S A SEXT TO JESUS!" Sarah screamed. "Stop it, OH MY GOD, STOP IT!"

She covered her ears and ran back into the bedroom, but I chased after her, almost slipping on the dildos.

"*Would I be woman enough for You? How would it feel to be flesh to flesh? I will do whatever it takes to please You, my Lord.*"

"I WILL KILL YOU!" she yelled. "Stop, please, I can't handle any more. And what the fuck? I thought she was a lesbian."

I closed the notebook. Even I couldn't take any more erotic Jesus fan fiction.

. . . .

It's been a few years now since we dumped mom at the home and completely forgot all about her. Just kidding, just kidding. Steve, Daisy, and I get up there to see her as often as we can. When Covid hit and her nursing home completely locked down, I worried that my mom would become isolated and lonely, so I called her a lot during those days. One time when we were on the phone, she was distracted, talking as much to someone else as she was to me.

"Hi, honeyyyyy!" she said to someone, practically singing. And then, "Oh hellllooooo!" to someone else.

Chapter Eleven

NEVER TOO BIG TO FAIL

After a few months, it was clear that my mom was fine at the nursing home. Actually, she was more than fine. She was *thriving*. She had a ninety-six-year-old roommate named Dorothy who she was *obsessed* with, and whose daughter would sit with them for hours discussing books or eating lunch. She also had a Jamaican nurse named Sarah who she had a crush on.

And when the pandemic-era restrictions started loosening up, she had an endless stream of friends visiting her. It was such a relief knowing that my mother was being well taken care of and wasn't lonely . . . and I am a little ashamed to admit that, eventually, we sort of stopped going to see her in person.

I know, I *KNOW*, this makes me a monster, but hear me out. It's not totally my fault! In a way, knowing that she was so well taken care of decreased the urgency to see her. Like, she was *happy*. Why rock the boat?

Also, we'd been driving to Cape Cod to see my mother for years . . . and it is grueling. Google Maps estimates it to be a five-hour drive door-to-door. However, since we became parents, we have never, EVER, done this drive in fewer than eight. This, I've found, is for several reasons. First, there's the child-aged traveling companion. I love my kid. Like really *LOVE* my kid. But there's something about sitting in a car that turns her into a urination factory. There have been trips to the Cape where we've had to stop FIVE times for her to pee. Sometimes we don't even pull off the highway anymore—we just pull onto the shoulder and let her squat next to the car. Because who has the time to find indoor plumbing when we STARTED THIS DRIVE FOUR DAYS AGO. We even let her poop on the side of the highway once, and I will not be judged by you.

Speaking of *you*, not visiting my mom is partly your fault. Well, at least those of you who drive. We need to talk about the wild abandon with which some of you are approaching your vehicular responsibilities. I have never in my *life* been slowed down by as many traffic accidents as I have in the past few years. Nothing can convey the rage I feel when I'm cruising along at a perfectly normal speed, blasting the Indigo Girls' self-titled album, because obviously, when suddenly the Google Map turns from blue to yellow to red, and TWO HOURS gets added to the trip time. All because some SUV with one (!) passenger has rear-ended a Volvo. Like, where are you all going in such a hurry?

And not to blame everyone but myself here, but at the end of this grueling journey is about an hour of "quality time" with my mother. I mean, she's not physically strong enough to leave the facility, so Steve, Daisy, and I end up just standing around her bed for a while as she shouts for every passing resident, nurse, or handyperson to introduce us—or, in most cases, reintroduce us. And she does these introductions with a dual purpose: to announce to everybody that Steve and I are homosexuals, and to point out how physically attractive my husband and daughter both are.

"Sandra!" my mother would shout as the nurse delivering lunches walked by her room. And then a louder "SANDRA!" when Sandra pretended not to hear her.

"Yes, Pam?" Sandra said good-naturedly, ducking her head in.

"I wanted to introduce you to my son Patrick and his *hussssssssss-band*, Steve," my mother would say, drawing out the gayest part of the sentence as long as her breath would allow. And then just to make sure Sandra got it, she'd add, "They're married," as she wagged her finger back and forth between us. Yes, it's lovely having a proud parent, but, like, this is the exact reason why my *gay mother* was the last person I came out to back in my teenage years: we can't launch a Pride parade every time I walk into the room!

"Hi," I said, waving at my good friend Sandra, who I was now meeting for the fourth time.

"Isn't Steve so—"

"—handsome, yes," Sandra said, finishing my mother's sentence. She knew the drill.

"And this is their *daaaaaaaaaughter*, Daisy," mom went on, emphasis on "daughter" to highlight that we weren't regular gays; we were special gays—*parent* gays. And then: "They adopted her through *foster care*," which she said solemnly to really drive home how *truly special* we are.

"What a beautiful little girl," Sandra said, beating my mom to the punch in a comedically brilliant over-the-top monotone. My mother nodded knowingly. Sandra winked at me and then went back to her food delivery.

Though my mom could go on all day, this routine usually lasts about an hour. The last time we were there, Steve called it when Daisy reached for Mom's roommate's bedpan. "Time to go," he announced as he scooped up our kid and handed her to grandma for a kiss good-bye. We'd put in a sixteen-hour round-trip drive for a sixty-minute visit. I love you, Mommy Dearest, but there has to be a better way. (Derek, that's a brilliantly placed callout to the gayest movie of all time. When you finish *The Golden Girls* catalog, Google "no wire hangers," and it'll take you right to it.)

But even if my family skipping visits to Mom wasn't *totally* my fault, I realized at some point that we'd waited too long for a return. So, I began investigating our non-driving options. There are no direct trains between New York City and Cape Cod, so that was out. But what about flying? JetBlue could get us from New York to Hyannis, the main "city" on the Cape, but it would require a six-hour layover in Boston. Slightly better than driving, but not by much.

Then something interesting popped up in my KAYAK search. A company called Private Air was offering direct service from JFK in New York City to Hyannis on a private flight. Takeoff to touchdown, the total travel time was forty-six(!) minutes. That seemed impossible. For context, that's a shorter amount of time than it takes just to get from our apartment to the car-rental place before the nightmare drive even starts!

Now to be *very* clear, flying private is not only an option that I never really even knew existed before that moment—who am I, Taylor Swift?—it was also never *ever* a financial possibility for Steve and me.

To give you a sense of our financial life at this point—and I'm gonna tread very lightly here, because Steve does *not* like it when I talk about our finances—just after the daycare days, my and Gillian's podcast, *True Crime Obsessed*, started to pick up momentum and therefore attracted advertisers. And not to brag, but, like, we're great at ads. To this day, nobody sells a mattress or a meal kit better than us. Sometimes I truly believe that, professionally, I was not put on this earth to make a podcast, but rather to tell you how much I love HelloFresh, and the universe just gave me the podcast as a vehicle to do it. Anyway, within six months or so, we'd both been able to quit our jobs to focus on making the podcast full-time. And I know I just wrote that like a regular ole sentence, but honestly, that was when I started to question reality for a little bit. Like, in what universe does one go from dragging themselves every day to a job they hate to making a decent living goofing around into a microphone in their living room with one of their new favorite people on the planet? To me that felt like some *Truman Show* shit—you know, the movie about the guy who doesn't know that his whole life has been a reality show that the entire world is watching? It seemed like a legitimate possibility that this was happening to me because *this* couldn't be real. Plus, I mean think about it, I'm *ridiculous*—I'd make great TV. And then we found *even more* success when we started making bonus content through Patreon.com. You know Patreon—it's like a sex-free OnlyFans. So, for a few bucks a month, listeners can support the show and in return get access to extra episodes. We were going so strong at this point that Steve was able to quit his job and become our full-time business manager. Which we desperately needed. Because Microsoft Excel.

So for the first time in our lives, we were becoming financially comfortable-ish. But enough to justify taking a private fucking plane to see my mom for an hour? *No way Steve is going to go for this*, I thought, as my finger, um, slipped and totally accidentally clicked the "reserve now" link. Whoops! Look, I wasn't committing to anything, just getting an estimated cost, right?

The price was daunting, but much less than I expected. I mean, I was expecting it to be forty million dollars, so what the hell do I know? It was a lot. But it would spare Steve sixteen hours of listening to Paula Cole albums in the front seat and "Let It Go" on a loop from the back seat. He might just go for it.

"Babe," I said, too excitedly, still staring at the computer.

"Oh God, what did you do?" he said. He gets genuinely nervous when I'm left alone with a computer and a credit card for too long.

"Should we take a private plane to go see my mom this weekend? I mean we have to go. So it's either an eternity in the car or FORTY-FIVE MINUTES on a plane."

He was quiet for a second. *Oh my God, he's actually considering this.*

"How much?" he asked. I turned the computer to show him. "Huh," he said, "not as much as I would have thought."

"I know," I said. "No wonder Taylor Swift takes her private jet to the grocery store."

"Fuck it," he said. "Let's book it."

. . . .

I gotta say, clicking "confirm" on a private jet rental felt pretty baller. I mean, I'm the same person kids at school used to draw living in a dumpster—remember "Becca's Family Inside"? Well, Becca's Family's Inside A PRIVATE FUCKING PLANE NOW, BITCHES!

I will say, the whole thing did make me feel the tiniest bit guilty. Mostly because I'm mildly obsessed with Greta Thunberg—you know, the teenage climate-change activist who, rather than flying, sailed a freaking boat from Europe to a meeting in the US to leave a lighter carbon footprint. Like, Greta is amazing. I was not like that as a teenager—hell, the only thing I cared about at that point was waking up early enough to make sure the family dial-up internet could download pictures of Marky Mark Wahlberg in his underwear before the rest of my family woke up. Priorities, Greta. I should have known better by now, but instead, here I was paying in glaciers and the lives of polar bears just to not have to listen to nine hours of my kid's iPad.

The day before our flight, I got a voicemail from a woman named Heaven who "had some questions about our flight."

This was concerning.

Even though I fly a lot, I'm still a bit of a nervous flier. I am always—*always*—looking for signs from the universe in the days and hours leading up to a scheduled flight that I shouldn't get on it, because this is the one that's going down. I was once supposed to meet a friend for lunch at O'Hare in Chicago where we both randomly had connecting flights. My first flight had been delayed so I got to O'Hare much later than expected, and as I jogged through the terminal to make my connection, I texted her, "Can't meet, running to my gate!" It wasn't until I got to my seat and checked to make sure the text had gone through that I discovered I had actually texted, "Can't meet, running to my fate." Running. To. My. *FATE*. I gay-gasped. That was no chubby-thumbed accident. That was the universe letting me know that this was it. We were all going to die.

Somehow, I survived that one. But now, here was the sign, plain as day: *Heaven* had called. With some *questions*. About our *flight*. We were goners.

When I called the customer service number back and got her on the phone, I was nervous. And when I'm nervous, I make bad jokes.

"Thank you for calling; this is Heaven."

"Oh, PHEW!" I said. "I was afraid I called the other place!" I cringed. Please, everyone reading this, imagine the cricket noise.

" . . . Excuse me?"

"Oh . . . ugh . . . sorry, nothing," I stammered. "It's just . . . I'm a nervous flier, so when, um, *Heaven* called with *questions*, I just, like . . . shouldn't Heaven be waiting until *after* the plane crashes to begin my interrogation? . . . Hahahahaha."

Dead silence. And then, "Sir, I just need to know how many bags you'll be bringing."

She didn't think I was funny. Another bad sign.

The next morning we headed to JFK airport for our flight. And, yes, it felt great to be able to drive past all the terrible little Arrival and Departure areas to the back side of the airport where people who fly on private jets go. People like us! We parked our car in front of this little building, and an unbelievably hot young guy came out to greet us. He was built like a Hemsworth brother, tall and strong with impossibly thick hair and a jawline you could plow a field with. Normally, I'm bored by tall, good-looking, straight guys who aren't Ryan Phillippe—sorry, Derek—but in this instance, I was thrilled to be in the presence of a Tarzan. Like, somehow, if things started going south at 30,000 feet, he'd be able to keep the plane in the air by the sheer force of his hotness.

He introduced himself: "Hi, I'm Jason. I'm gonna be your pilot today. Do you need any help with your bags?" Oh my God, he had perfect teeth.

"No thanks, we're good," I said shyly. Actually *demurring*. Oh my GOD, was I fluttering my eyes too?

"Okay, well if you need *anything*, I'm your guy."

"How about a promise to hold me if we go down?" I said before I could stop myself. Steve just rolled his eyes.

"Now THAT is a promise," Jason/Tarzan said as he squeezed my shoulder. And suddenly I was hoping for disaster. Sorry, family, I'm not passing up an opportunity to die in Tarzan Hemsworth's arms.

Tarzan walked us into the little lobby and said we were good to go whenever we wanted. I used the bathroom and grabbed four complimentary minibags of Cheetos and stuffed them in my coat pocket. Because when you have the opportunity to take free Cheetos, you do it. Like a goddamn adult. Okay, I was ready to fly.

We walked out onto the tarmac and there we saw her: our gorgeous private jet. It was bigger than I expected! It looked like it could easily seat eight or ten people comfortably, plus a flight attendant who, I was sure, would *insist* that I go ahead and have that 8 AM screwdriver. "Be bad!" I imagined her saying while pouring me a double. *We're on a private jet! Why not!* And truly, I saw Greta Thunberg's annoyed little face again, scowling at me, shaking her little head. She was right; this was overkill. But there was nothing to do about it now but enjoy the trip. *Sorry Greta, Patrick's gonna be a little bad!*

As I started to walk toward the jet, Tarzan grabbed my shoulder and shouted, "No! No!" with genuine panic in his voice. "That's not your plane!"

"It isn't?" I asked.

"No! That plane belongs to the Kingdom of Saudi Arabia! One of their princes just landed," he explained. "THAT'S your plane." He pointed at a little prop plane. It looked tiny and terrifying, about the size of a moving van or a big taxi. Or a hearse. Definitely no room for a naughty good-time flight attendant to goad me into boozing it up. *Damn you, Greta.*

Tarzan must have seen the look of concern on my face, because he said, "Don't worry, this thing has the most top-of-the-line lawn-mower engine of any plane I've ever flown." He said that with actual pride. He was trying to be reassuring and charming, but failing.

And then it all made sense. We hadn't booked a private *jet*; we'd booked a private fucking *crop duster*. That was why it was so much less expensive than we'd imagined. Tarzan Hemsworth was about to fly us to the Cape in an airborne John Deere. Wherein, I'm assuming, there was no bar.

Before we could change our minds, he hustled us over to the little plane.

"Okay, what do each of you weigh?" he asked.

"WHAT?" I shrieked. This question was a . . . surprise, and, frankly, rude, Tarzan. "Would a . . . cumulative number be acceptable?" I asked, not exactly psyched about the prospect of giving this human protein shake my personal stats. Also, *why* did he need to know this? Was it possible that if we gave him too high a number, this thing wouldn't get off the ground? Or worse, would Tarzan politely *try* to get us airborne and a few minutes after takeoff the plane would be like, *oh fuck this*, and down we'd go?

Tarzan chuckled. "I just need the specifics to calculate who needs to sit where," and then he launched into a bunch of math stuff that definitely seemed like a "Steve problem," so I stopped listening.

The entire passenger space was smaller than the back seat of a station wagon, so we filed in and Steve configured us thusly: I was seated directly behind Tarzan's pilot seat, facing away from him, with Daisy in the seat next to me and Steve across from her. We spent a few minutes taxiing on the runway, during which I said three "Hail Marys" while Daisy held and stroked my hand, and then we were off.

And the very second the wheels left the ground, I realized I had to pee. With some urgency.

A quick side-note about my . . . constant need to urinate. I have been plagued with this my entire life. I've been to doctors and specialists, and everyone has assured me that my penis and all of the things on the inside of my downstairs work just fine. Better than fine in some instances, WINK. There's no reason, I'm told, that I should have to go as often as I have to go. This uncontrollable urge has snuck up during Broadway shows and car trips, inconveniencing people and ruining special moments many times over. Once, during a *True Crime Obsessed* live show in Chicago, we were about three minutes into the show when the need to pee hit me like a needle to the dick. I had to go NOW. This was a ninety-minute show that had me rolling around on the floor, jumping up and down, and chugging a pint of water, which I pretended was vodka. Because I am hilarious. There was no way I was going to make it. So I announced to the audience, and to my startled, then annoyed, but ultimately not-that-surprised co-host Gillian that I was taking a quick break. (We'd been making *True Crime Obsessed* for over three years at that point, so she was very used to my bladder-related needs.)

"Nature calls! Be back in three minutes!" I yelled as I dashed off the stage.

"But girl, you peed literally four times before we got out here," Gillian shouted into her microphone, making it a bit. And then, "Soooo . . . anyone have any questions?"

Apparently two-thirds of the audience took my pee break as their cue to run back to the bar for another drink. Our listeners love a cocktail. We ended up breaking that venue's bar record that night, which is 100 percent a true story. You're *welcome*, Chicago.

The point is, in all of those instances, I've had a bathroom to go to. Looking around our lawn-mower plane, it was clear that if there was no room in these six square feet for a booze-pushing flight attendant, there was also no room for a bathroom.

In my defense, I had peed literally six minutes earlier, just before nearly inciting an international incident by accidentally boarding the Prince of Saudi Arabia's plane! And also in my defense, I had been expecting a *jet*. With multiple (!) bathrooms, probably even a shower! I hadn't planned for a bathroom-less flight situation. Remember how I gave my daughter shit for being a urination factory on road trips at the top of this chapter? I never pee on those trips because I *plan* for them. I stop all liquids—even bourbon, if you can believe it—twelve hours before we get on the road. But today, anticipating *luxury*, I'd been drinking coffee all morning. And water. Lots of water. I'd even brought a half-full bottle of Fiji Water with me on the plane.

After about two minutes in the air, the situation was getting worse. I leaned across to Steve and said, "I have to pee." I don't know what I was expecting from him at that moment. Could he conjure a bathroom? Steve had lived through this with me a thousand times. He didn't make an annoyed face or roll his eyes; he just took a deep breath and said, "Well, we'll be there in an hour," and leaned back to continue doing his *New York Times* crossword puzzle. In pen. Which will never not be incredibly sexy.

I sat back and tried to listen to a podcast, hoping to take my mind off of my issue. *It's only an hour.* I knew half of my problem was probably just mental: If the plane HAD a bathroom, I probably wouldn't even need to pee. But since it didn't, I *really* HAD to pee. It was all just a mind game! But actually, I really, really did have to pee. The podcast wasn't helping. I took off my headphones and tried to breathe.

Daisy sat next me, obliviously watching videos on her iPad. *Watching Elsa melt her frozen kingdom into rivers and oceans and waterfalls was NOT helping.* I was starting to panic. We were ten minutes in and I felt like I was going to give birth though my penis. Could we land this thing somewhere for me to pee? Tarzan was too hot for me to ask.

I started kicking the bottom of my seat with my foot. Steve looked up from the crossword. I shook my head. *Am I about to fucking cry?* There must be a plan for this, right? I can't be the only person who has ever had to pee on one of these shitty little planes, right? Is there some sort of secret urinal? I frantically looked around but didn't see anything.

Steve motioned to me, nodding toward Tarzan, indicating I should ask him. "STOP IT, STOP IT," I whisper-growled, through gritted teeth. The idea of Tarzan looking back here and seeing us talking about him or in any way involving him in this pee-mergency was out of the question.

In as calm a voice as possible, I said, "Hey Tarz . . . er . . . Jason? Any idea how much longer till we get there?"

We had taken off like ten minutes ago, so he sounded surprised. "Oh, like another hour or so? Everything okay?"

"Yup!" I said, cheerily. I was fucked. Turning to Steve, I said, "Every second feels like I'm dying."

"You're not going to die!" Steve whisper-yelled back. Was he about to slap me? Was I becoming hysterical? It sure seemed like it. He was mad, but he was also in problem-solving mode. He picked up the half-full bottle of Fiji, guzzled the rest of the water, and shoved the bottle into my hands.

My eyes widened. "NO" I scream-whispered.

"IT. IS. THE. ONLY. OPTION." Steve scream-whispered back

Oh my God, he was right. *Okay*, I thought, *this is happening*. I was about to fill this bottle with my own human waste. And if Hot Tarzan saw me, I'd jump out of the fucking plane to spare us all the humiliation.

But first: How do I pee into a bottle without my daughter—who was sitting six inches from me—noticing? I could already see how this trip would go from "Daddy, remember when we flew in that fancy private plane to go see grandma" to "Daddy, remember that time I watched you desperately piss into a bottle and was never able to take you seriously as an authority figure ever again?"

I unzipped the hoodie I was wearing and covered my crotch with it. The problem now was I couldn't really see what I was doing. It's not like these Fiji Water bottles are made for peeing into. One's penis does not fit neatly INSIDE the neck. No, this was a situation that required AIM. And if my aim was off, if I didn't shoot straight or was unexpectedly jostled, I'd be spraying ALL OVER MY FAMILY.

Also, the chair I was sitting in was angled in entirely the wrong way. It was permanently reclined so that my pelvis was tilted, creating a blockage that I wasn't sure I'd be able to overcome. There's a reason there are no recliner toilets; it's not the way the body works. I tried to stand, but that was impossible. I tried to lean forward while standing but couldn't pull that off without calling Tarzan's attention to my NOW EXPOSED PENIS.

I settled back into my seat and then pushed myself to the edge of it. It still wasn't an ideal position, but it was going to have to do, because it was go time. I glanced around the cabin. Daisy was still absorbed in her iPad. Tarzan was totally oblivious. Steve was staring directly at me. "Look away," I whisper-screamed. And he did. Just in time for my somehow perfectly aimed Number One. Sweet, sweet relief.

As soon as we landed, I ran right into the airport bathroom, threw the bag in the trash, and PEED AGAIN.

When I came out of the bathroom, Steve asked me what I did with the tote bag. "I threw it away!" I said. I thought he'd be happy to never have to think about it ever again.

"Patrick," he said, uttering words that only a gay man would ever say. "That was my FAVORITE tote bag." It seemed insane to me that he was still so attached to a *New Yorker* tote bag with my human waste in it. But because I love him so much, I walked back to the bathroom, dug the bag out of everyone's disgusting bathroom trash, threw away the bottle, and brought the filthy, beloved tote out to my husband.

If there is a lesson to be learned here—and after that sort of humiliating torture, there better be, right?—for me it's to stay grounded. Like, literally. Drive, don't fly to see your mother. And if you have to fly, just go with everyone else. Nobody needs a private jet.

Chapter Twelve

GIVE MY REGARDS TO BROADWAY

For all the epic mistakes I've made in my life, one of the things I have managed to absolutely nail is surrounding myself with people who generally say "yes" when I excitedly present them with my big ideas. Really, I'm just talking about my husband, Steve, and podcast partner, Gillian. Take a private plane to go see mom? Sure. Write a book exposing the fact that I have basically no idea what I'm doing in business or in life? Go for it. Take our little podcast to Broadway even though it's never been done before and might bankrupt our little success story? LET'S DO IT!

In April of 2020, *True Crime Obsessed* was set to make its Broadway debut. We'd been touring with the show for years, and the Broadway idea had started out as a joke—like, can you imagine *Two Theater Kids Make It to Broadway on Their Own Terms!* But the bigger

"Mom, who are you talking to?" I asked, annoyed.

"It's Teri and Gerree and Sue," Mom said. "They came for a visit."

"What? How?" I asked. "I thought the nursing home was completely locked down—that you couldn't have any visitors."

"No visitors *inside*, Patrick dear. They're outside my window next to my bed."

"Really?" I asked.

"Yup, once a week or so, some assortment of girlfriends come and stand outside the window and wave at me. We can't hear each other, but they stay for a bit and keep me company."

I could 100 percent picture the scene. My mom, comfy and cozy in her bed. Her friends, a crew of smiling older lesbians with short, sensible haircuts, all piled around each other waving into my mom's room. They couldn't really communicate, but it didn't really matter; it was the *being there* that was important. Lesbians, man—they will always show up. It wasn't perfect, but, resourceful as always, it was what they could do for now: create a Closed Window Social Club.

the podcast got, the more seriously we started to take the idea. And then one day, I just said, "fuck it," and started calling around to various Broadway theaters to see if this dream was even a possibility. That's how you get on Broadway, right? You just call Broadway up and see if they'll take you?

This spontaneous recon mission on my part was mostly an exercise in patience. Which, like most forms of exercise, I'm not great at. And in fairness, I get it, here's some queeny gay guy cold-calling your multimillion-dollar theater organization inquiring about renting your historic and iconic building for something called a . . . *podcast*? I can understand how that would raise some questions. But once we got past the basics of what a podcast *is* and that, no, unfortunately, there is no place you can watch it, I guess I just wasn't prepared for the level of dismissiveness I'd encounter. The abrupt, pre-hang-up "not interested," or "you must have the wrong number," or, my favorite: "Ma'am, do you know how much renting a Broadway theater costs?" and then click. What was a one-time future Newsie to do?

Ultimately, the people at Second Stage Theater—a nonprofit theater company who had just completed their purchase of the Hayes Theater on Broadway—were patient enough to hear me out. Barbara, the lady on the other end of the line, even knew what a podcast was and was *obsessed* with true crime, so we had our in. And after meetings and site visits and contract negotiations, the deal was made, and tickets went on sale. In the spring of 2020, *True Crime Obsessed* would be the first podcast to ever play Broadway. Nothing could stop us now!

You could hear the sarcasm there, right? Of course little did we, or anyone, know that a once-in-a-century pandemic that would shut down the world was barreling toward us and would, at least temporarily, derail our Broadway plans.

. . . .

I think that everyone probably remembers the moment they realized that the world was going to change. Maybe they were told to go home from work and didn't return for over a year. Or maybe they saw their first person wearing a mask and thought, *What the hell?* My moment of realization was, predictably, very, very gay.

The date was March 12, 2020, my dear friend and fellow podcast host Ellyn Marsh's birthday. I wanted to take her out to dinner, but I'd forgotten to make a reservation . . . because I forgot it was her birthday . . . because, as Ellyn will attest, I'm a self-centered son of a bitch. We took our chances at our favorite spot in the theater district, Joe Allen, and we were able to get a table at 6:30 PM. AS. WALK. INS.

Crazy, right? Normally, if you walked into Joe Allen at 6:30 PM, an aging gay man would *delight* in humiliating you in your pathetic attempt to, you know, eat dinner. He would use insider theater jargon to explain why you won't be seated for hours: "Unfortunately, the Dolly mat ended late today and the Sweeney curtain is at seven! So we're FULLY committed." (Translation: the *Hello, Dolly!* matinee ended late and *Sweeney Todd* starts at seven, so there won't be any tables for a while.) At a table behind him, Bernadette Peters would whisper something mean about you to her tablemates, and they would all chuckle. Even Audra McDonald. It's enraging. But it's also gay heaven.

Anyway, a half-empty Joe Allen ninety minutes pre-theater could only mean one thing: People were too scared to go out. The world was shutting down. Within the hour, all Broadway shows were suspended indefinitely and we got an email from Daisy's school that all schools were closing and going remote, whatever that meant.

When I got home from dinner that night (yes, Ellyn and I stayed at Joe Allen for a meal even as the world seemed to be ending around us—what, was I *not* gonna have the steak tartare?), I took one look around our six-hundred-square-foot, three-room apartment and told my husband, "Fuck this, we gotta get out of here."

I just didn't see how we could stay. Daisy would be doing virtual school from home. Steve would be . . . her teacher from home? I'd be making the podcast full-time, also from home. It was impossible. We had no outdoor space and the city was literally locking the playgrounds. New York City seemed like the most terrifying place to be in the world outside of Wuhan fucking China; we needed to get the hell out of it for a while.

And look: Call me a drama queen all you want, but I'm not exactly what you'd call "in shape" or a person who had, like, "taken great care of his body" or someone who "ate vegetables regularly." Turn the book over and look at that author's photo. See? At the time, what we were hearing about Covid made it sound like anyone who didn't run marathons regularly would die gasping for air in an emergency room hallway. No fucking thank you. So we scooped up the kid, booked an Airbnb "cottage" in the wilds of Massachusetts, and ran to the local Avis where we got—and I'm not kidding—the second-to-last rental car in Midtown. New Yorkers were peacing the fuck out because New Yorkers love New York, until there's any reason to leave it. Then it's everyone for themselves.

· ·

As has been well established, I love a good, strong, earthy lesbian vibe. And let me tell you, this Massachusetts Airbnb cottage was like the Rosie O'Donnell of Airbnb getaways. We're talking the full

Melissa Etheridge, people. From the bohemian mandala tapestries that adorned the walls, to the DVD collection (*A League of Their Own*! *Bound*! *Thelma & Louise*!), to the pickled canned vegetables in the refrigerator—I think I genuflected when I saw that. These weren't just regular lesbians. These were lesbians who canned their own asparagus. Hardcore respect, ladies. My lesbian mother, and hers before her, would be very, very impressed.

Though the cottage was perfect, within a few days of our sapphic Massachusetts adventure, I was beginning to feel like we had made a terrible mistake. The place was everything the listing had promised it would be: isolated, secluded, *miles from your nearest neighbor*. Like how long can an extreme extrovert be expected to live under those conditions? I need people! Community! Three Dunkin' Donuts on the same block, all of which have my order memorized! I was going insane from boredom. New York still seemed risky, but at least there you got to see your neighbors for two minutes a day when we all stuck our heads out our windows to bang pots and pans for the healthcare workers. (Remember that?) Playing country mouse wasn't going great. And so I guess it's no surprise that by the end of that locked-down first week, Steve was getting sick of me.

Things sort of came to a head early one morning in the kitchen. We were staring into the fridge trying to figure out how to contain the smell coming from the six jars of pickled garlic on the top shelf. And I was nonchalantly telling Steve about the ghost I'd seen the night before. This story is 100 percent true and normally would be the kind of thing that would terrify me, but it was the first bit of excitement I'd had all week and I was dying to tell him about it.

"So it was like three in the morning or something, I woke up and went into the kitchen to get a glass of water and there was this older man—early fifties, maybe? So not *super* old, but a bit older—sitting *right there* at the table."

"Uh-huh."

"It was *crazy*—he was wearing this, like, old-time army uniform? And he was just *sitting* there. Oh! *And* he had a green cap pulled down over his eyes like he was asleep. Like, he was a GHOST, but he was ASLEEP . . . it was WILD."

"Right."

"And it was weird, because at first it felt totally normal, right? I guess because we're still new to the cottage and it was the middle of the night, I was kind of out of it, so I was just like *Oh, huh, yeah there's a fully formed stranger sitting at our table*, and by the time I realized how weird it was, I looked back and he was *gone!*"

Steve had stopped even courtesy responding. He wasn't being rude, really; it's just that Steve does not believe in ghosts. For him, when you die, you're just worm food in a box. (Romantic!) I, on the other hand, have always imagined that some fabulous yesteryear gay icon, like Judy Garland or Ethel Merman, would greet me on the other side with a clipboard. After handing me a cocktail, but before anything else—before reuniting me with long-lost loved ones, taking me to the magical grizzly bear field where you are encouraged to hug, ride, and nap with the bears, or teaching me how to haunt my childhood bullies—she would go over the list on her clipboard, giving me all of the *real* answers to earthly mysteries I'd obsessed over as a human: *Who killed JFK? Who the hell WAS D.B. Cooper? DID ALIENS HELP MAKE STONEHENGE?* TELL ME, JUDY! The point is, I believe in the afterlife, and I believe that it's going to be fabulous. A gay bar on every Heavenly corner. Steve knows this about me, of course, and he humors me because he loves me and gets me. And, if we're being honest, on good days he's even *amused* by me. So on occasion, he'll tolerate something as ridiculous as a very true ghost story. But today was not that day.

No, instead, today he'd continue impromptu homeschooling our rambunctious, dyslexic six-year-old who was *intensely* struggling with remote learning, terribly missing her friends, and just wanting to play with her fucking hamster. So rather than indulging me and the ghost story, he moved on to the other piece of stress I'd saddled him with: the Broadway show. I tend to do this to him—come up with some big idea, get super excited about it, and then, like, check in with him from time to time as he plans and executes the whole thing. I'm delightful.

"So I've been thinking, maybe this pause of who-knows-how-long could actually be good for the show. Like, if we're gonna be the first podcast on Broadway, maybe we should put some thought into it, you know, make it special."

"Huh," I said. I knew what he meant. I mean, we'd put a *ton* of thought into the idea of being on Broadway and making a little history, and, like, who we wanted at the after-party . . . and stuff. But as for the show itself and making *that* special? Yeah, *that* we hadn't really thought about. I mean, our live shows are great and they're really, really funny. So as far as Gillian and I were concerned, we were just gonna, like, do what we'd been doing in theaters around the country, except on a Broadway stage, in our *fancy* jeans.

But Steve was right. Gillian and I were theater kids who'd once dreamed big of being on Broadway. Somewhere along the way, we'd given up that dream, but here was a rare opportunity to get our goddamn dream back! Cue *The West Wing* theme music because we ARE going to be on Broadway! On OUR terms! With OUR show! WE DO NEED TO MAKE IT FUCKING SPECIAL!

"FUCK, YES!" I screamed, startling both Steve and Daisy who, I'd forgotten, had not taken that mental journey with me.

"Are you okay, Daddy?" Daisy asked.

"I'm great, sweetheart," I said. And I was great. Because, when this nightmare pandemic situation was over, I was gonna be on BROADWAY! And Steve was gonna make it special. And I would check in on him from time to time to see how that was coming. Because I *am* delightful.

. . . .

We stayed at the lesbian cottage for a full two months before we couldn't take it any longer. The isolation, not to mention the stench of pickled . . . everything, had gotten old.

We headed back to our beloved New York City where we stayed inside, ordered *and then washed* our groceries, and drank copious amounts of alcohol. (No joke: in New York City, liquor stores were deemed "essential services"—as essential as grocery stores and, like, hospitals.) When the world finally FINALLY began opening back up in the fall of 2021, Broadway theaters slowly began reopening too. In October, when Second Stage Theater reopened, we reached out to pick the date for *True Crime Obsessed LIVE on Broadway:* April 11, 2022. That meant we had a little over six months to make our scrappy little live show *sparkle* for The Great White Way.

Our plan was to do a big Broadway opening number and a big Broadway closing number with our regular live show sandwiched in between. And so we needed a director—someone with vision. Someone who could take the *True Crime Obsessed* themes of humor, authenticity, and compassion, swirl that together with our over-the-top personalities, add just the right amount of G A Y, and then birth two perfectly executed dance numbers to open and close the show.

We took a few meetings and it quickly became clear that there was only one person who could get that done on our tight timeline: Bob Bartley. Bob directs an annual benefit for the organizations Broadway Cares/Equity Fights AIDS and New York City's Lesbian, Gay, Bisexual & Transgender Community Center called *Broadway Backwards* in which leading performers from Broadway shows perform songs not traditionally sung by their gender. The show is fun and hilarious and sentimental and very, very G A Y—the exact mixture we were looking for. Bob was our guy.

Bob came over to our apartment to meet with Steve, our co-producer Natalie Grillo, Gillian, and me. Over wine and cheese, we discussed ideas for the show. The meeting was going great, and at 8 PM, Steve excused himself to put Daisy to bed. Not five minutes later, she emerged from her room and walked into the living room where we were all still sitting.

Now, I don't know exactly what I was expecting from our seven-year-old—maybe some sort of impromptu "So Long, Farewell" number to charm our guests before quietly putting herself back to bed? We are homosexuals after all; isn't this how people expect our children to behave? But what we got instead was Daisy, staring blankly at no one in particular, tilting her head, and saying, "Daddy, I know you're gonna die soon."

This was . . . unexpected. Here we were, five adults, several glasses of wine and a full cheeseboard in, making plans about Broadway dreams coming true, and we're interrupted by this . . . death threat? Or a prophecy? And anyway, *which daddy*?

A note about my daughter: She is a truly beautiful and spirited little girl. But in the wrong light and in a situation where her daddies have rushed her off to bed without brushing her hair, Daisy can look quite a bit like that little girl from *The Ring* who crawls out of the TV to kill everyone or whatever. Backlit by the fireplace, her face barely visible under shadow and an unruly mane of hair, she repeated herself: "Daddy. I know you're going to die soon."

WHAT THE FUCK WAS HAPPENING? Was she planning to kill me? She did seem to be staring right at me. Had Satan come to her in a dream just to let her know, or had she simply done the calorie math on the daily pizza I'd been consuming for the two years of quarantine? Oh, and the bourbon. And the ice cream. *Oh my God, was I going to die?*

Whatever the reason, this kid was killing the vibe of our very first post-pandemic wine-and-cheese party. No gay should have to stand for that. She had to go. I scooped her up and sort of jogged her down the hallway to her bedroom. (Exercise! See: I'm going to live!) As we went, Daisy became hysterical: "Why do you have to DIE?? Why, Daddy? Why do you have to diiiiiieee?!?"

When I emerged from Daisy's bedroom a while later—having finally been able to convince her that I was, at least, not dying *that* night—neither Bob nor Natalie, to their credit, made mention of the bizarre interruption. And I'd love to be able to tell you that I made an instant decision to change my dietary ways, just in case the kid was right, but we all know that didn't happen. In fact, I started wondering *when* our guests would leave. Daddy was ready for second dinner.

Bob accepted the job despite the bad omen. One of the notes from our meeting that he seemed to really take to heart was the request to gay up our show a bit—you know, really make it . . . twinkle, which he did to the tune of six beautiful Broadway chorus men: Adam, Michael,

Ryan, Jake, Waldy, and Colby. These guys were beyond attractive. Their eyes sparkled like animated porn actors or Disney princesses. Their bodies were formed of pure athletic muscle. And I don't know if I'm allowed to say this or not, but some of them had the kind of asses that turn people gay. I'm afraid the Republicans are right on this. In the case of these boys' asses, it *is* a choice. You *can* be turned by asses like these.

Even though we'd been planning the show for months, when it came to rehearsal with the dancers—because this was a legit Broadway contract with very strict rules around the number of hours allowed for rehearsal time—we only had a week. For me, the rehearsal week was the most magical part of it all, truly rivaling the actual *doing* of the show on the Broadway stage. I thought a lot about Seventh Grade Me that week. Remember him? The one who dressed in full *Go Ask Alice* drag to lecture his classmates about how they should just say no? As you can imagine, Seventh Grade Me had had a tough time. I was chubby, I wore Coke-bottle glasses, and at the time I was *really* leaning into emulating my mother's lesbian aesthetic, both in clothing and hairstyle. My mullet knew no limits. Seriously, look at me!

Yeah, kids made fun of me. The worst part was that I just wanted to be a part of a group so badly, but I couldn't seem to find my place. I didn't understand why it was so hard; I was fun, I was nice, but the other kids wouldn't give me a chance. And so on the way to and from school every day, I'd sit alone on the bus and crank up the original Broadway cast recording of *Tommy* or *Miss Saigon* on my, wait for it, Sony Discman. I'd imagine that I was Future Me and the school bus was actually a New York City bus taking me to a rehearsal for the big Broadway show that I was starring in. I would close my eyes and imagine the smells and sounds of New York and really *truly* experience the excitement that Future Me felt about his life and New York and Broadway. It seemed, somehow, both possible but also almost too far away to be real or in any way attainable.

But now, here I was, fucking doing it! Just before I walked into the first rehearsal for our Broadway show co-starring ME, I took a quick second for my seventh-grade self. *You did it kid*, I thought. Here you fucking are.

. . . .

Because of how Broadway rental agreements work, we weren't able to get into the theater until the day of the actual performance. Even then, because of all the union rules, prior to the show, I wasn't allowed to be anywhere near the stage without an official escort—which meant that we could look at the stage, but we couldn't go on it until our technical rehearsal started. So, imagine my delight when, about two hours before tech, our assistant stage manager, Mike, came to the dressing room to get me.

"I need to bring you down to the stage so I can show you where your props are on stage left," he said.

"Oh my God," I screamed, "we're actually going onto . . . the stage?"

"We are!" Mike said with a smile.

I followed Mike down three flights of stairs, through a zigzag maze of hallways, and then suddenly, without any warning, Mike told me to take a step up, and then there I was, standing on the Broadway stage. *My* Broadway stage . . . at least for the night. Now, before I tell you the obvious anecdote about how hard I cried in that moment, let me just remind you that it had been a very long and isolating pandemic, and now, to be in a theater, a place designed for the sole purpose of bringing people together, and to have the reason they were coming together that night be for something that I helped make—oh and, ANNNND that this was the theater; nay, the very STAGE where the groundbreaking, unabashedly gay, seismically important play *Torch Song Trilogy* had premiered in 1982—and now, tonight, I was going to tread the same boards as the show's writer and star, the iconic Harvey Fierstein? Yeah, that hit me all at once and I became hysterical. So, you know, a little notice next time, Mike.

We checked our props, ran our tech, and before we knew it, the stage manager, Kaleigh, called "places." Gillian and I would be entering from opposite sides of the stage, so we grabbed a quick private moment in the wings before going our separate ways.

"We did it, girl," she said, as she hugged me.

"We did it, girl," I said back. And then, predictably, I was crying again.

When I got to my pre-opening spot on stage right, I could hear the audience fewer than one hundred feet from where I was standing. The energy coming from the house was electric—every single person in the room knew what that night meant to us and I could feel the love they were beaming our way. I was suddenly overcome with excitement and nerves, and I started jumping up and down to try to burn off some of the energy. The whole thing felt so enormously *big* to me in that moment—the responsibility to pull off something historic and freaking FUN. I couldn't wait to get out there and do it. Tonight we were going to make the theater gods proud.

And then, boom, the lights dimmed and we were off and running.

The show opened with a reimagined version of "Cell Block Tango" from the musical *Chicago*. The choreography was Fosse inspired. (He's a famous choreographer, Derek. Don't worry, we're almost done.) It was intricate and sexy and the boys executed it flawlessly. Interspersed throughout the song, Gillian and I popped in, playing various characters from the documentaries we'd covered on the podcast, and the audience went wild. It was the perfect, perfect opener.

The middle part of the show—the documentary recap part—was seamless. And then the real drama came at the end. The show ended with a fake-out for the audience. I put up a slide of Gillian and me, each from our respective high school drama club days. We thanked everyone for coming and being there to witness our Broadway dreams come true. Then, just as we were saying goodnight, our emcee, Tony-winner James Monroe Iglehart, came busting in from the wings.

"WAIT, WAIT, WAIT, WAIT!" he said. "This is Broadway; you don't just say 'goodnight.' You have to send the people out with a big finale!"

We feigned shock. *Little Ole Us? But how? Wherevah could we learn, like, the choreography?*

"Get out of here," he cajoled. "We've got a costume change for you offstage."

So we exited to slip into our jackets for the big showstopping finale: "Give My Regards to Broadway."

We had rehearsed this finale for hours and hours. Whereas the opening number was all comedic bits and wigs and impressions, the finale was actual fucking choreography. Admittedly, most of it fell to the boys—Bob had been kind (or, like, smart) enough to stage it so Gillian and I were mostly danced *around* while we *oooooo'd* and *ahhh-hhhh'd*. But still, for a couple of non-dancers, there was a lot of shit for us to know, including the mechanics of a Rockettes-style kick line at the climactic moment of the song. And now that everything else had gone perfectly, I was going to be damned if I was going to let down the Rockettes. Do they even let you still be gay after that?

So as I stood there in the wings, feverishly counting my eight counts, getting ready to make my entrance, I felt a firm hand on my shoulder; it was Josh, the co-choreographer.

"Patrick," he scream-whispered. "I can't find Gillian and this is VERY fucking important."

"What?" I scream-whispered back, "she's on the other side of the stage! She enters stage ri . . ."

"LISTEN TO MEEEE—" he hissed. I had never seen Joshey like this. "You HAVE to remember to tell her that at the end of the finale, right after the kick line, she has to exit UPSTAGE right instead of downstage right."

I nodded. "Okay," I said, even though I had no idea what he was talking about.

He grabbed me by both shoulders and stared directly in my eyes. "PATRICK. This is very fucking important. We had to re-stage the dancers, so if she doesn't exit UPSTAGE, she will be CRUSHED BY THEM."

"Okay," I said. "I got it!" I absolutely did not have it. I know this sounds like a simple enough direction, but with all my own closing number choreography swirling around in my head, and the general overload of adrenaline coursing through my veins, I just couldn't focus. Gillian was a goner.

I ran out onto the stage at the appointed time. We did the finale, and it was perfect. I even aced the kick line, which had required light jumping, which I'd resented.

The final moment of the number called for Gillian and me to be pulled onto different dancers' laps as we tossed our arms into the air for the final pose and the audience was instantly on their feet. I'd promised myself—PROMISED MYSELF—that I would not get lost in that moment. That I would feel it, be present for it, so that I would always remember it. So that's what I was focused on as the music played out and we all stood and prepared to run off the stage to get ready for curtain call. And then Josh's warning came back to me. Fuck! I leaned into Gillian and tried to scream, "You have to exit UPSTAGE instead of downstage!"

"WHAT?" she yelled back.

"You have to EXIT—"

Too late. The curtain-call music started, Gillian hopped off her dancer's knee, and off she went, downstage, most likely to be accidentally trampled to death by our six beautiful dancers. *Ah*, I thought, *what a way to go.*

. . . .

Good news: Gillian didn't die. The dancers, consummate professionals that they are, realized that Gillian hadn't gotten the note and corrected the situation themselves.

Gillian and I quickly changed into our street clothes and then met the theater's security team by the stage door. This was another moment I'd dreamed of my whole life: walking out the stage door of a Broadway theater to take pictures and sign *Playbills* for a gathered, adoring crowd. The question was: Would anyone be out there?

The security guard asked us if we were ready. We looked at each other and said yes, and then the nice man opened the door. Before we could even see the streetlights, we heard the thunderous screams of hundreds of people who were waiting to congratulate us. And so into the adoring throng we went, adoring them right back.

It's funny how you become what you become, right? I had to pursue a dream—to be a great actor, to open a daycare, to become the world's most efficient executive assistant—to eventually find the dream job I have now. It couldn't have happened without the world's most supportive husband pushing me in the right direction. And who can even explain my good fortune in linking up with Gillian? Together we've created something special, something people love. What a life we've built! What a community!

But I also think that I had to be bad—*really bad*—at a bunch of things to find the thing I'm good at. In a way, isn't the lesson here that you kind of have to open a daycare and then close it in a week? Not to be too grandiose about it, but don't you sort of *have to* get chased by a few knife-wielding neighbors? Shouldn't we all let our podcast partners almost get crushed by some incredibly fit Broadway dancers? Hmmm?

Gillian and I do a lot of Q&As at our live shows, and one of the most common questions I get is some version of this classic: "If you could go back and tell your younger self something, what would it be?" And my answer is always: Fail more. Fail bigger. Fail *every freaking day* if you can. Sure, it's painful in the moment, but it's always been in those painful moments that I've learned and grown the most. Plus, failing at something means you tried—you took a chance. You were brave in some way. And *that* is to be fucking celebrated.

So go forth and fail, people. And may all your failures be epic! But before we part ways, I must ask you to do me one small kindness on your journey: If any of your many future fails include you falling into a pool, or, like, being unable to stop yourself from sliding down an icy driveway when you were out one morning just trying to get the goddamn mail—if you aren't seriously hurt *and* somehow managed to capture a video of it on your phone—please, *please* immediately upload that shit to Instagram. You might not have learned anything from the fall or grown in any way, but, come on, those videos are hilarious. They're actually little gifts to humanity and proof that the world is a better place when we all take ourselves a little less seriously.

ACKNOWLEDGMENTS

To paraphrase the immortal words of Kim Basinger receiving her Academy Award, I was only given thirty seconds and I would just like to thank everyone I've ever met in my entire life. But more specifically:

Steve and Daisy, thank you for making the time and space for me to write this book and to do all the other things. It's all only worth doing because I have the two of you to do it with and for.

My collaborator, Doug Moe, thanks for guiding me through this process with humor and persistence and for finding me funny AND for being funny. This would have been a very different book without you—probably long and boring and serious. Like *Moby Dick*. The world didn't need another *Moby Dick*. Also, does writing the acknowledgments mean we're done? No? We're never done, are we? Please go and buy and read and tell your friends about Doug's hilarious book: *Man vs. Child: One Dad's Guide to the Weirdness of Parenting*.

My agent, Oren Rosenbaum, my brother, you are stuck with me forever. Thank you for guiding my career so expertly and for bringing so many good things into my life. I love you endlessly. Also, remind me to introduce you to carbs. You're gonna *LOVE* potatoes.

Byrd Leavell, thank you for believing in me and this book. Writing this has been a dream come true!

Natalie Grillo, this (and so many other wonderful things in my life) would have never happened without your tireless enthusiasm and support! Never leave us!

The team at BenBella Books, especially our editor Alyn Wallace—thanks for your insight and for going on this journey with us!

My mom and sisters, Sarah and Becca—thanks for letting me share our story! And thanks for always loving and supporting me no matter what.

My friends who are family—there are too many of you to name individually, but you know who you are. Thanks for believing in me and laughing at my dumb jokes. But honestly, some of you should have tried harder to talk me out of the daycare. You also know who you are.

ABOUT THE AUTHOR

Patrick Hinds is the co-creator and co-host of the hit true crime/comedy podcast *True Crime Obsessed*, where each week he and his co-host, Gillian Pensavalle, give their take on a true crime documentary with humor, heart, and sass. With over two hundred million downloads, *True Crime Obsessed* is one of the most popular podcasts in the world. *TCO* made history by being the first podcast to play live on Broadway in 2022.

In 2020, Patrick and his husband, Steve Tipton, created the Obsessed Network, where they oversee the production of the hit podcasts *Murder in Alliance*, *Obsessed With: Disappeared*, *I Think Not!*, *Strange and Unexplained*, and *Crimes of the Centuries*. They also co-created the popular annual true crime fan convention Obsessed Fest.

Longtime fans will remember that Patrick is also the creator of several esteemed Broadway podcasts, including *Theater People* and *Broadway Backstory*.

You can follow him on Instagram and TikTok: @patrickhinds_.